TALK with ANGELS

How *to* Work *with* Angels *of* Light *for* Guidance, Comfort *&* Healing

Elizabeth Clare Prophet

Summit University Press®

Gardiner, Montana

TALK WITH ANGELS
How to Work with Angels of Light for Guidance,Comfort and Healing
by Elizabeth Clare Prophet
Copyright © 2014 Summit Publications, Inc.
All rights reserved

For information:
The Summit Lighthouse, 63 Summit Way, Gardiner, MT 59030 USA
1-800-245-5445 / 406-848-9500
TSLinfo@TSL.org
SummitLighthouse.org

Library of Congress Control Number 2014947405
ISBN: 978-1-60988-243-3 (softbound)
ISBN: 978-1-60988-258-7 (eBook)

SUMMIT UNIVERSITY ☙ PRESS®

Cover design by Nita Ybarra
Interior design by James Bennett Design

This book is excerpted from the lecture series "How to Contact Angels—Your Guides, Guardians and Friends," by Elizabeth Clare Prophet.

Go to our website for selected audio recordings of the angel meditations, songs and mantras found in this book (and many others): www.SummitLighthouse.org/TalkWithAngels.

20   19   18   17   2   3   4   5

TABLE *of* CONTENTS

Angels *and* You

1

ANGELS *and* YOU

*A*ngels are very real and personally present in our midst. They are all around us. When we commune with the angels, they bring us to a higher plane of consciousness. If we invite them into our lives, they will assist us in the work we do. Angels have a mission—God created angels to be our guides, guardians and protectors.

Every angel who comes to us comes as a messenger. In fact, the word *angel* comes from the Latin *angelus*, meaning "messenger." Angels convey messages of love, joy, peace, teaching, warning, protection. Have a listening ear and a receptive heart and you will begin to hear and sense their direction in your life.

The author of Hebrews tells us that God "maketh his angels spirits, and his ministers a flame of fire."[1] God created the angels out of his own fiery being. They are not flesh-and-blood beings. They are beings of fire, extensions of God's presence, and he made them so that he could dwell with us through his angelic retinue.

HEAVENLY CAREGIVERS

God created the angels before he created us. He knew we would need heavenly caregivers, so he created angels to be just that. He planned it so that they would be in place and ready when the time came to bring forth his sons and daughters.

Each and every angel who comes knocking on your door, from the least to the greatest, is the repository of a special grace or gift that God himself is sending to you marked "personal" with your name on it. When you open your door and your heart to an angel, be ready to be filled with a sacred essence from God formulated especially for you.

My interaction with the angels has shown me that they tend our bodies, console our spirits, invigorate our minds, and restore our souls. They deliver God's word and his intercessory works to us and they convey God's prophecies and warnings, his comfort and enlightenment, his exhortations and spiritual admonishments.

ANGELS *and* ARCHANGELS

Think of the manifest presence of the one God as the Great Central Sun, the hub of light at the nexus of the Spirit-Matter cosmos. Think of the T'ai Chi, the great symbol of Taoism, the two halves of the whole, as representative of the plus and the minus, the Spirit-Matter cosmos, or the Father-Mother God.

Out from this blazing, dazzling Central Sun, which is so vast that we cannot even have a sense of co-measurement with it, come shafts of light that become angel forms as they descend to earth. As sunbeams are to the sun, so are angels extensions of the living presence of God. And the greatest of these are the archangels and archeiai. When you stand in the presence of an archangel or an archeia,* you are standing in the presence of God. I'll say more about this in a moment.

Angels have a multitude of offices and functions that are divided among the heavenly hierarchies ruled by the seven archangels. Thomas Aquinas defined angels as the guardians of men, the messengers of God who deliver communications of lesser importance. He said that the archangels are those angels who carry to man the most solemn messages entrusted to them by God.

Archangels are the captains (the hierarchs) of the angelic hosts. They preside over the seven rays, seven light-emanations of God's consciousness. Archangels are God's architects. God uses them to draft the plans for his projects and execute them. They are cosmic builders and designers in the grandest sense of the word. Archangels arc to our minds the divine blueprint for every endeavor.

The archangels are cosmic beings who predate us by millions of years. They were our first teachers. There is no field of learning in which they do not excel.

All archangels are healers. They come as master surgeons to repair bodies and mend the rents in the garments of the soul. With the Elohim, the co-creators of life and form, they also have power to create and uncreate life. The archangels are extraordinary beings—nothing less than God personified in form as God's grace and majesty and power.

EMBODIED ANGELS

All angels worship Jesus Christ as the incarnation of God— all angels, that is, except Lucifer and his bands. The ancient

An archeia (plural archeiai) is the feminine complement of an archangel.

myth of the fall of angels is true. These angels would not bend the knee before the Son of God. Instead they made war against the Woman and her Manchild. So, as it is written in Revelation 12, Michael the Archangel cast them out of heaven. Lucifer and his bands lost that war and swore eternal enmity against the Christ as the True Self of every son and daughter of God.

But there is another chapter to the story of the Great Rebellion that is not recorded in Revelation. When the good angels saw that these fallen angels went about the earth making war against the children of God, they said: "We will volunteer. We want to go down and take on human form so that we can teach the people about the treachery of the rebel angels and protect the children of God from their evil intent."

God allowed those good angels to also take embodiment. And so they are in every race, amongst every people, and in every nation. Some serve as wonderful teachers, comforters, or ministers, and they love us, protect us and tend to our needs in many ways.

Haven't you ever said, "Oh, he's an angel" or "She's an angel" when you have seen someone good and caring and selfless? That is the nature of angels. They are here for only one purpose: to help the rest of us make it Home. The apostle Paul was inspired by his own direct encounter with the angels and he gave us this reminder: "Be not forgetful to entertain strangers: for thereby some have entertained angels unawares."[2]

ANGELS *and the* SON *of* GOD

Who is the Son of God and what is his relationship to the angels? The author of Hebrews writes:

What is man, that thou art mindful of him? or the son of man, that thou visitest him?

Thou madest him a little lower than the angels; thou crownedst him with glory and honour, and didst set him over the works of thy hands:

Thou hast put all things in subjection under his feet. For in that he put all in subjection under him, he left nothing that is not put under him. But now we see not yet all things put under him.

But we see Jesus, who was made a little lower than the angels for the suffering of death, crowned with glory and honour; that he by the grace of God should taste death for every man.

Because Jesus was born of the flesh, it is said that he was "made a little lower than the angels." You see, prior to the Great Rebellion of Lucifer, angels had never descended to the lowly estate of the flesh; they had never occupied bodies of flesh such as we wear. So until the rebel angels fell, all the angels of heaven worshiped the Son of God and ministered unto him in all of their various capacities and callings from God.

Hebrews continues:

For it became him, for whom are all things, and by whom are all things, in bringing many sons unto glory, to make the captain of their salvation perfect through sufferings.

For both he that sanctifieth and they who are sanctified are all of one: for which cause he is not ashamed to call them brethren.[3]

The author of Hebrews seems to know very well that when Jesus sanctifies us, we are then no different from Jesus—for he has given us the sanctification of himself. That is why Jesus calls us his brothers and sisters.

Jesus has made us his equals. That is what the author of Hebrews believes, what he tells us. The very fact that Jesus calls us *brethren* establishes you and me as Jesus' equals—equal in opportunity, equal in inner resources, equal in the ability to walk in his footsteps and perform the same works that he performed. That is why Jesus himself gave us the promise, "He that believeth in me, the works that I do shall he do also; and greater works than these shall he do; because I go unto my Father"[4]—*all* of the works, all the way to the resurrection and the ascension.

Because Jesus raised the sons and daughters of God to be his equals, Paul was able to tell the Corinthians, "Know ye not that we shall judge angels?"[5] And that means the fallen angels.

When Jesus Christ had fulfilled his final incarnation on earth and ascended to the throne of grace, *then* he was crowned with glory and honor above all the angels of heaven. And because Jesus, the captain of our salvation, chose to make each of us his own, when we fulfill the requirements for the ascension in our final incarnation on earth, we will also ascend to heaven.

YOUR DIVINE SELF *and the* SON *of* GOD

The mystery of our relationship to the Son of God and the angels is revealed in the three figures in the Chart of Your Divine Self. You are represented in the lower figure, surrounded by the flame of the Holy Spirit, the violet flame. The violet flame is God's gift to us for the erasing of our errors, our sins.

The middle figure in the Chart is the figure of the Mediator. He mediates between us in our sinful, or karmic, state and God, of whom Habakkuk wrote, "Thou art of too pure eyes to

behold iniquity."[6] The Christ alone can go before the throne of God. And he alone can descend right into our temple and counsel us.

This Christ Presence is your Holy Christ Self. That is the term I use for that middle figure in the Chart. It can also be called the Higher Self, the Real Self, the Higher Mental Body, the Inner Man of the Heart, the Inner Guru, the Inner Buddha, and the voice of conscience.

Jesus Christ came to demonstrate for us what is that Christ Self and how that same Christ can be manifest for each one of us. This is the relationship we have to the Son of God. The Son of God is the living Christ. This word comes from the Greek *christos*, meaning "anointed." The Christ is one who is anointed with the light of God. And this is not exclusive to Christianity. Every avatar who has ever come in all ages has been anointed with that light.

Our individual Christ Presence is like the Christ Presence of Jesus. It is shown on the Chart as being above us, because we have not yet prepared our temples to fully embody that Christ. But there are moments and days and hours of our lives when, through prayer and communion and intense love that pours through us for others, we feel sublimely touched by that presence. That Christ Presence draws so near to us it overshadows us, and we experience the fulfillment of Jesus' promise that "if you will love me and love my Father and keep our commandments, we will take up our abode in you. We will live in your temple. We will speak through you, walk through you, live through you."[7] This is the goal of our walk with God in this life.

The upper figure in the Chart is God's presence individualized for us. God placed a replica of himself with us. There is only one God. But that one God has so loved you and so loved me that he placed this magnificent presence of himself over us and within us. It is the same presence that God revealed to Moses as the I AM THAT I AM. We call it the I AM Presence.

How many Gods, how many I AM Presences? If we each have one, there is still only one. In time and space we see duality and separateness. But there is only one God, personified in each and every one of us.

Our relationship to the angelic hierarchy is through the Son of God—not only as Jesus Christ but as that Christ Self personified through each one of us. Through that Son in whose hands God has placed the dominion of all worlds, we have contact with the I AM Presence and we have contact with the angels.

ARCHANGELS *of the* SEVEN RAYS

Surrounding the upper figure in the Chart of Your Divine Self are the seven spheres of the great causal body. These seven spheres (shown in cross-section in the Chart) correspond to the seven rays, to the archangels who serve on those rays and to the seven major chakras in the body of man.

God has placed these chakras, or spiritual centers, in your body to hold light and energy. They are positioned along the spinal column and operate at subtle levels. Each of the archangels corresponds to one of your seven chakras. The archangels use those spiritual centers to deposit light in your being.

All angels have a tremendous aura. And the archangels, who are over the other orders of angels, have an aura that is extraordinary in size. You can readily sense their presence in your feeling world—you pick up feelings of love, hope, faith, encouragement, support. This is because the way they help us is to use their auras to transmit or transfer to us a portion of the tremendous light that they have from God.

Sacred fire of God is not hot. It is cool except when it touches discord or misqualified energy. When you come into the aura of an angel or when he comes into your aura, he will not leave you as he has found you. And so by his very living, flaming presence you may feel the alchemy of transmutation, of the consuming of old stubbornness and pride. It is a humbling experience, profoundly humbling.

As you become familiar with the seven archangels and archeiai and the rays on which they serve, you will soon learn how each one can assist you with the development of one of your seven chakras and the qualities associated with it.

Archangel Michael and Faith—Angels of Protection

Serving on the first ray is Archangel Michael, the Prince of the Archangels, and Archeia Faith, his divine complement. The color of this ray is a brilliant royal blue, corresponding to the outermost ring of the causal body and to the throat chakra. Blue is the color of power, of government, of perfection and of protection.

Archangel Jophiel and Christine—Angels of Wisdom

The archangel and archeia of the second ray are Jophiel and Christine. This ray corresponds to the yellow band of the causal body, which surrounds the white light at the center. The second ray is yellow, the color of illumination and wisdom; it corresponds to the crown chakra.

Archangel Chamuel and Charity—Angels of Love
Chamuel and Charity are the archangel and archeia of the
third ray. This is the ray of love, the pink ray, and it corresponds
to the third band of the causal body and to the heart chakra.

Archangel Gabriel and Hope—Angels of Purity
Serving on the fourth ray are Archangel Gabriel and Archeia
Hope. The color of this ray is white, and it corresponds to the
base-of-the-spine chakra and the center core of the causal
body. It is the ray of purity, of the ascension, and of the Divine
Mother.

Archangel Raphael and Mary—Angels of Healing
The archangel and archeia of the fifth ray are Raphael and
Mary, the Blessed Mother of Jesus Christ. Mary is known as the
Queen of Angels. This ray corresponds to the green band of the
causal body and to the third-eye chakra, the inner-eye at the
brow. Green is the color of healing, science and mathematics.

Archangel Uriel and Aurora—Angels of Peace
On the sixth ray are Archangel Uriel and Archeia Aurora. This
ray corresponds to the fifth band of the causal body, which is
purple and gold flecked with ruby, and to the solar-plexus
chakra. It is the color of peace, ministration and service.

Archangel Zadkiel and Holy Amethyst—
Angels of Freedom
The archangel and archeia of the seventh ray are Zadkiel and
Holy Amethyst. The seventh ray is the violet ray, the ray which
releases the violet flame. This ray corresponds to the seat-of-

the-soul chakra, located between the base chakra and the solar plexus. Violet is the color of freedom, transmutation, forgiveness and alchemy.

SPIRITUAL NOURISHMENT

When you give prayers or mantras that are comfortable for you, or when you exercise or do yoga, the angels can nourish your chakras and replenish them and increase the light in your temple. The light that you carry energizes your form and enables you to resist diseases and illnesses. The light that you carry gives you the energy to accomplish your mission and your divine plan, so protect the light in all of your chakras.

There are many ways of squandering light. One of the ways that light goes out from an individual is by their putting attention on so many things in the world and forgetting to put attention on God for a few moments, even fifteen minutes a day.

When you put your attention on God, you open a track through your third eye, through your heart, through your devotion, through your inner seeing. You actually open a highway to heaven. As you send your devotion over that highway, God receives your devotion, multiplies it, and returns it to you as spiritual nourishment for your body and soul.

GETTING *to* KNOW *the* ANGELS

When you are familiar with the angels and their various offices and you trust them as your guardians and guides, you can feel absolutely comfortable talking with them anytime, anywhere. You can be comfortable walking with the angels, calling to them, giving them assignments, asking for their assistance in difficult personal matters and in matters of global concern. You can ask the angels to take command over matters such as problems in the environment and all of the situations that are so deplorable and so heartrending around the world.

How many of us feel helpless before these world events, as though we could do nothing about them? That sense of helplessness probably affects everyone on earth at some time, and it can be profoundly frustrating. We cannot control calamity in the earth, in our own backyard and sometimes not even in our own kitchen. That's why we need the angels. That's why God created angels.

LEARNING *from the* ANGELS *in* THEIR ETHERIC RETREATS

The angels have retreats in the heaven-world, as do Elohim and other beings of light. The retreats are well above the pollutions of earth on a level called the etheric plane. These etheric retreats are older than the earth and are centers where tremendous light is released. This is why people make journeys to special places on the earth—they sense and can access the vibrations of the beings of light who make their abode there.

The archangels' retreats are open to souls of merit and your soul can travel there during sleep. Just before you retire at night, pray to Archangel Michael and his legions of angels to escort you to realms of light to attend classes in these universities of the Spirit.

You may not remember what you have studied in one of the archangels' retreats, yet your soul knows. And little by little, the information trickles down to your mental awareness. Sometimes you might say, "I have an idea," and it is a memory of something you picked up in those inner schools of learning.

MY FIRST ENCOUNTERS *with* ANGELS

Eighteen was a turning point in my life. I was leaving home to go to college, about to start finding my way in the world. I was looking for my path.

I was very serious about pursuing God, and at every available moment I would take my Bible, go to my room, and ponder the words of Jesus. As I read those words and communed with my Lord, he would say in my heart, "Everything that I have taught is not there." When I would listen to the ministers preach on Sunday, Jesus would say in my heart, "Everything that I have taught is not there."

I had found the Christian Science Church when I was a child and it taught me more about God and myself and Jesus than I could learn anywhere else. I also had a great affinity for the Catholic faith. I loved the statues, I loved to light the candles, and I used to pull my mother into Catholic churches and ask her if I could light a candle and kneel before the Blessed Mother. Whenever I went to church I always came out feeling filled with the light of God, yet not always able to translate the meaning of that light.

One bright Sunday morning I came out on the front steps of the Christian Science Church in my hometown, Red Bank, New Jersey. As I was standing there in the beautiful sunshine, I found myself face to face with an angel. It was the most tremendous moment in my life. I had never experienced anything like it.

I was taken aback, because I was not expecting to see an angel standing before me, much less an archangel. It was Archangel Gabriel. I knew it as I knew my own soul. He allowed me to see him by quickening my inner sight. I felt his powerful presence and I felt my mind lock into the mind of

God through his intercession. He made me feel that this was altogether natural.

I was having a conversation with him, and at the same time I was one with God. It was as though he transmitted to me a message from God "spherically"—that's the only way I can describe it. It was a sphere of all-knowingness, of self-knowing fused with my own sense of self-awareness in God.

As I look back upon it, I realize that this was made possible through the rings upon rings of the aura of Archangel Gabriel. They seem to have served as an antenna, stepping down a communication from a very high plane to my level. In the split second it took for me to receive the higher awareness that Gabriel conveyed, I heard myself say out loud, "Why, I have to make my ascension in this life!"

I was astounded by the words that came out of my mouth. No one had ever taught me that I was supposed to make my ascension in this life. I had always been taught that only Jesus made the ascension. But indeed it is for everyone. And for a second I knew that I had experienced the all-knowing mind of God that my Sunday school teachers had talked about.

The interchange couldn't have taken more than sixty seconds. But I was suspended somewhere else. I had glimpsed heaven and Archangel Gabriel. That one glimpse would carry me for a lifetime until my cup and my mission were full.

As I look back on that moment, it's amazing to me that although I was a part of orthodox Christianity, I was receptive to a thought transfer from the mind of an archangel telling me precisely why I was here and what I was to accomplish. I knew it then and I know it now, that the ascension is the goal not only for my life but also for yours.

ASCENSION, *the* GOAL *of* LIFE

I knew then that this was a message I had to tell the whole world, anyone and everyone who would listen. I saw that there were people all over the world who were ready for that message, that acceleration, who could graduate from earth's schoolroom in this life, but who needed the rest of Jesus' teachings that had been lost or deliberately left out of the Bible. Not only do the archangels teach you how to attain the goal of the ascension; the ascended masters also teach how to attain that goal.

The ascended masters are people like you or me, but they've done two things that we have yet to accomplish: become the masters of themselves—their minds, their emotions, their lives—and balanced at least 51 percent of their karma. As a result, they have accelerated into higher dimensions of light. They have passed through the ritual of the ascension, hence they are called "ascended" masters.

Earth is a schoolroom, and we ought to be moving along and graduating. There is another schoolroom waiting. We get from here to there through the ascension, a process that itself has steps we must take.

Many years after my experience with Archangel Gabriel, I took the opportunity to ask my Christian Science teacher about the ascension. To my amazement he just passed it off as something that automatically happens at the conclusion of a life that is lived in God. But I knew that the ascension doesn't just happen. We have to define it as a goal and we have to understand how to get there. It doesn't happen "just because you're a good person," as he assured me it did.

There are requirements and initiations. The soul has to

pass through the trial by fire, and then there is the lifelong challenge of karma. If you ask Gabriel, he will communicate to you through your mind or heart, through a certain inner impelling that this is the goal of your life.

My encounter with Archangel Gabriel sent me on a relentless course to know God face to face. I had come that close to Gabriel. Moses had communed with God on the mountain. Jesus Christ, Zoroaster, Krishna, Gautama Buddha, Confucius and many of their disciples had communed with God. I knew that everyone in this world had the right to talk to his God one on one, face to face, and there was a burning desire in my heart to tell everyone that very story.

It doesn't matter what you have done, who you have been, what sins you have committed. God will take all of that and let the flame of the Holy Spirit pass through it. Don't accept the label or the condemnation that you are a miserable sinner and can never overcome that state of sinfulness. You are the beloved of God this day.

You may have sinned but you are not a sinner. You are a child of God, a son or a daughter of God. In you dwells your Higher Self, that living Atman, that inner Christ, inner Buddha. It is the inner light, and that is your true identity.

You are made of "God stuff," and that spirit of the living God is upon you and in you and focused through your chakras. The angels are here to tell you about it, to quicken you, to accelerate the light that you already have and to give you more.

"A MULTITUDE *of the* HEAVENLY HOST"

That meeting with Archangel Gabriel was not the first time I had experienced angels. Earlier in my eighteenth year, I was water-skiing down the Navesink River one beautiful day, going out toward the ocean. Suddenly I realized that I had entered another dimension. Midst the blue sky and billowy clouds I saw not thousands but millions of angels—"a multitude of the heavenly host."

I saw that they were my friends, brothers and sisters, spiritual companions from many centuries rejoicing with me that in this age all of our bands would have the opportunity to attain union with God. I knew that I was not alone in my quest. I had known these cohorts of light forever, and they were joining me, cheering me on.

In that experience on the river, I knew that I was called and that my Lord would make known to me the particulars of my calling in this life. And I knew that I would never be alone, because the angels would always be with me.

MY CALLING

In 1961 God did call me to be a messenger for the archangels and the ascended masters.

I met Mark Prophet in 1961 when I was attending Boston University. He came to deliver a lecture and I saw an angelic presence over him. That evening, as a messenger, he delivered a dictation from Archangel Michael.

This was the first time I had ever heard a human being as the instrument for the Word, the presence and the vibration of an archangel. It was a stupendous moment in my life. I could feel all the atoms of my being repolarized to God. I could feel the influx of light in my chakras. There was no questioning the testimony of the presence of an archangel, because how could one ever feel such tremendous power of

God except in their presence?

Mark Prophet became my husband, my teacher, my dearest friend. I was with him for twelve years, and then he took his leave of this octave.

Through Mark Prophet as their messenger the ascended masters trained me and anointed me to deliver the word of God in dictations in the tradition of the Hebrew prophets. Mark, who had received his training ten years before me, was my tutor "in the flesh." He drilled me day after day for three years in the rigors of the ascended masters' discipline. I count this very personal instruction under the masters and Mark as the greatest blessing I have ever known. Without it I would not have been ready to deal with the challenges I have faced throughout my mission.

Many people ask me what my training was all about. They always think that I was trained to take a dictation, but there really is no training to receive the dictations from God through the Holy Spirit.

What was my preparation, then? I was trained in the work of Thomas à Kempis, *The Imitation of Christ*. I was trained in how to subdue pride and all of the other vices we are heir to. I was trained in how to give the comforting word, how to talk to people and not belittle them, not to utter anything that would tear from a living soul the sense of the presence of God. I was taught the disciplining of the emotions and the mind. I read certain books.

But what finally came to my heart as the point where I could be trustworthy to bear the mantle of messenger and take dictations was the putting together of a spiritual path of love and discipline. It is a path of understanding the difference between pride and humility, boldness in the Lord and absolute tenderness toward every part of life. The training on this path goes on through a lifetime.

Mark and I have taken hundreds of dictations from the archangels, and I will be quoting from them here.

COMMUNING *with the* ARCHANGELS

DEVELOP A LISTENING EAR

How can you be more attuned to angels and their presence with you? How can you foster your contact with the angels?

One of the most important steps you can take is to develop a listening ear. Turn off the TV. Turn off the noise. Keep your mind open, not saturated with information coming at you from without.

Have a certain time of day when your home is silent, even if it's just before you retire at night. Bring your awareness to your inner ear and listen to God. And in preparation for hearing him, give prayers that you are comfortable with. Pray to God and his angels.

THE SPOKEN WORD

Throughout history and in ages for which we have absolutely no records—ancient Atlantis, ancient Lemuria, past golden ages on the earth that are but a dim memory in the unconscious—the traditional means of making contact with God and his emissaries, such as the seven archangels, has been through songs, chants, decrees, prayers, mantras, the intoning of Om and the Word of God.

Every religion has prayer and communion with God. When you commune and meditate in your chakras, opening these channels, you become filled with the light of the I AM Presence.

As you sing or pray to the archangels, you are talking to them. They hear you and answer on the return current of your devotion. As you give love and gratitude to them for their service to you and this world, you open a channel of contact. That is what loving God and his angels is all about—opening your heart to heaven so that the return current can bring the answer to your call and blessings without limit.

I have been taught that when you offer an invocation or prayer to the seven archangels, not only are the words important but there is a proper way to address such heavenly beings. The following prayer is an example. To begin communing with the seven archangels, you can give this prayer or compose one of your own.

Prayer to the Seven Archangels

O seven beloved archangels and archeiai, I call to you in this hour for the quickening of my heart, the quickening of my chakras, the quickening of the light of God within me. Come be with me, as I desire to know you and through you to know our Father-Mother God. I pour forth my gratitude for your protection of me, for your teaching, for your comfort and healing, for seeing me through each trial and victory, through the burdens and through the rejoicings of my life.

O God, I come before you in this hour with prayers for loved ones and those who suffer throughout the earth. I offer these prayers now and I know that you hear and answer instantaneously as this call does go forth.

It's easy to compose your personal prayers. Simply talk with the archangels about your concerns, your burdens, your hopes and aspirations. Ask for their help regarding specific issues for yourself, your loved ones and friends, and the city and nation in which you live.

Then listen and watch for answers and blessings.

How Angels Protect
You *and* Those You Love

2

ARCHANGEL MICHAEL *and* FAITH

God's love for us is so tender and so present that he makes this known to us in an especially personal way through his angels. Archangel Michael, who comes forth from the heart of God to minister to our souls, is known as the great intercessor and is the Captain of the LORD's Hosts.

Archangel Michael is a very special angel to us. For thousands and thousands of years Michael, along with his legions of light, has dedicated himself to the safety, security and perfecting of our souls, to protecting us, caring for us, sponsoring us, rebuking us, teaching us the way of God's holy will, and helping us to understand that we each have a blueprint in life, a divine plan.

Archangel Michael serves with Archeia Faith, his divine complement, and their legions of blue-lightning angels on the first ray, the ray of God's will. If you saturate your mind with a brilliant blue, the color of this ray, it will be a magnet to draw these angels to you.

We depend on the blue ray for the empowerment of God and for his protection. This ray also corresponds to government, to the economies of the nations, and to leadership, an important quality for everyone to develop. Follow Archangel Michael to develop a thrust for a purpose and a sense of direction. People will sense that you know where you are going. The first-ray chakra is the throat chakra. It takes the power of the spoken Word* to galvanize forces and to lead.

Michael and Faith and their legions have their retreat in the heaven-world over Banff and Lake Louise in the beautiful Canadian Rockies.

You can draw Archangel Michael's presence to you by playing his keynote, "Eternal Father, Strong to Save," which is also called "The Navy Hymn." The keynote of Archangel Michael's retreat is the "Soldiers' Chorus" from *Faust*, by Charles Gounod.

ARCHANGEL MICHAEL *in the* WORLD'S RELIGIONS

The name Michael means "who is like God." Some say his name is in the form of a question and was the battle cry of the angels who fought against the haughty Lucifer: "Who is like God?"

Archangel Michael has figured in Jewish, Christian and Islamic scriptures and tradition as the greatest and most revered of angels. Called Mika'il in Muslim lore, he is the angel of nature, providing both food and knowledge to man. In Zoroastrianism a parallel has been drawn between Michael and Vohu Manah, one of the Amesha Spentas, cosmic beings whose role corresponds to that of the archangels.

Exodus 3:2 is the first appearance of Michael in the West-

---

*Word *with a capital* W *signifies the dynamic, creative force of the universe, which releases the potential of God from Spirit to matter. "In the beginning was the Word."*

ern tradition. He is the "angel of the LORD" who appeared to Moses in a flame of fire out of the midst of a burning bush, which was not consumed. Exodus first says the angel of the LORD appeared to Moses, then says the LORD God himself spoke to him. It was Archangel Michael, the personification of the LORD God, who called to Moses.

In this passage, God reveals to us who we are. We are the bush that God made, and he has placed a fire in this bush— the all-consuming fire of God. The I AM Presence lives above us and in us. We are not consumed by this power, for God tempers his presence to our levels of identity. The fire that he has carefully enshrined on the altar of our heart is the divine spark, our original endowment from the beginning. It is a threefold flame of love, wisdom and power. Because you have that divine spark, that gift of immortal life, you can attain union with God. It is the key to your immortality.

GOD SENDS YOU *on a* MISSION EVERY DAY

Moses asked God, "When I come unto the children of Israel, and shall say unto them, 'The God of your fathers hath sent me unto you,' and they shall say unto me, 'What is his name?' what shall I say unto them?"

God said, "Tell them I AM hath sent you unto them. Tell them: My name is I AM THAT I AM."[1]

Think of yourself as the emissary of God in your town, city and home. Who sends you? Your Mighty I AM Presence, the living Presence of God, who walks and talks with you. God sends you on a mission daily to deliver his light to his people. He teaches you the science of prayer, the art of the spoken Word. He teaches you how to garner the light in your chakras so that when you meet those who are suffering and impoverished, who do not have the light in their spiritual centers, your cups will be full and you can pour from your own pitchers into their chalices. This is what you are called to prepare for each day.

Where would we be today had Moses not responded to the call of the LORD to bring his people out of Egypt? Half the miracle is that God, personified in Archangel Michael, appeared to Moses. The other half is that Moses responded and accepted his calling in the LORD.

YOUR CALLING IS UPON YOU

How will you respond when the angel of the LORD appears to you?

It's time to look at the sands in the hourglass and say, "What am I going to do with the rest of my life? How will I fill my remaining moments of time and space?"

How many people have absolutely locked in to their calling from God in this life? I cannot say that I have totally locked in to that calling, but I know my destiny. I know what I must do. And day by day I wait on the LORD for the direction for that day, that week, that month, that year so I can be certain to be at the right place at the right time.

God may call us, but how pitiful for us if we do not respond, if we say, "I have other cares, other things to do. I haven't yet resolved my psychology. I can't come now, LORD, but I'll be there next week or maybe next year."

You have lived before in many lifetimes. Although you may not totally believe in reincarnation, you may have had a sense of familiarity with something, a feeling of déjà vu. We have

lived before and we have come again. And this time we haven't
a minute to lose, because we are seeking ultimate salvation.

The inner meaning of the word *salvation* is "self-elevation."
We must see to our own salvation. God has put his Son in
place, his angels in place, his teachings in place and this wonderful world in place where we can study the lives of the saints
and great adepts of East and West. We have a choice to do
nothing, to do something, to do everything! We can say:

*This day I AM begotten of the LORD! This is the day the LORD
hath made for me and I will take it, I will run with it. This is the first
day of the rest of my life. I am going to be on fire for God every minute
and I am not going to sink back into the doldrums because of whatever is wrong with my body or my soul. My God is with me, the angels
are with me, and God has put me here for a purpose. I can overcome
and I will overcome all adversity!*

There is so much to do, and Archangel Michael will help
us and multiply our every effort ten thousand–times–ten
thousand. Let us not be one of those to whom the angels do
not appear because they already know we will have an excuse.
When they do not bring their message, it is so we will not
make the karma of rejecting it.

Have the angels passed us by because of our hardness of
heart, because we have said to God, "I am already doing
enough; don't ask me to do another thing"? What if that one
more thing will save a life, save a soul, catapult you out of a life
that is unproductive, unfulfilling, and catch you up in a mission that causes you to rejoice every day?

ARCHANGEL MICHAEL *in* JEWISH TRADITION

In Jewish mystical tradition Archangel Michael is identified with the angel who wrestled with Jacob, guided Israel through the wilderness, destroyed the armies of Sennacherib, and saved the three Hebrew boys in the fiery furnace.

The Book of Daniel describes Michael wonderfully:

> *At that time shall Michael stand up, the great prince which standeth for the children of thy people: and there shall be a time of trouble, such as never was since there was a nation even to that same time: and at that time thy people shall be delivered, every one that shall be found written in the book.*
>
> *And many of them that sleep in the dust of the earth shall awake.*[2]

When Daniel says "at that time," I believe he is speaking of a time like today. People are waking up, but what does he say about that? Some will wake up "to everlasting life, and some to shame and everlasting contempt." They awaken to their old momentums, to the results of the freewill choices that have formed their personalities and their identities—either one with God or opposed to God.

Daniel continues: "They that be wise shall shine as the brightness of the firmament." All will see them because their auras will be repositories of the light of the archangels, the light of God, which is the light of the I AM THAT I AM. This light cannot be hid. When this light lives in someone, it is like a gigantic fire blazing forth.

"And they that turn many to righteousness will be as the stars for ever and ever."[3] They will turn many back to the *right use* of the laws of God, the light of God, the name of God and the living Christ, who is the intercessor.

Your star is the star of your causal body, the intertwining spheres of light surrounding your I AM Presence. Paul wrote that one star differs from another star in glory.[4] Each of us has a causal body that is unique according to the good works we have done while living on earth.

This prophecy in Daniel is telling us that in this "time of trouble" *we need God.* We can't make it without him. We can access God through his archangels, whom he sends to be very close to us so that we will know that he cares and that he *will* deliver us from all darkness.

THE CAPTAIN *of the* HOSTS *of the* LORD

Michael is the angel who appeared to Joshua as he prepared to lead the Israelites in battle at Jericho. Here is the scene: This mighty archangel of the LORD is standing before the people.

And it came to pass, when Joshua was by Jericho, that he lifted up his eyes and looked, and, behold, there stood a man* over against him with his sword drawn in his hand: and Joshua ... said unto him, Art thou for us, or for our adversaries?

And he said, Nay; but as captain of the host of the LORD am I now come. And Joshua fell on his face to the earth, and did worship.

Joshua knew and felt the Presence of God in the presence of the archangel. If you saw an archangel of the LORD standing before you, you would fall on your face too! Joshua said to him,

---

*Angels are often referred to as "men" in the Bible.

What saith my lord unto his servant?

And the captain of the LORD's host said unto Joshua, Loose thy shoe from off thy foot; for the place whereon thou standest is holy. And Joshua did so.[5]

Because the archangels personify the Presence of God, the first request they will make of you is, "Put off your shoes. Put off the yoke of your karma, put off your human conscious-ness for the moment, and commune with God in the God-reality that is within you. You are in the presence of God. You can be transformed by that presence." Joshua obeyed, and the Israelites won the battle.

MICHAEL *in the* BOOK *of* REVELATION

Revelation 12 tells of Michael's role as the defender of the Woman clothed with the Sun and her Divine Manchild. The Woman clothed with the Sun is the figure of Mary, the Mother of Jesus, the one whom God selected to bear the Divine Man-child. The Woman clothed with the Sun also represents the female principle in all of us, our soul, the feminine potential of being in both men and women. The Divine Manchild is the Universal Christ, the Son of God—the real identity of the living Christ in Jesus and in each one of us.

Archangel Michael came to defend the Divine Mother and her Divine Manchild. He cast her adversary and all of his legions out of the courts of heaven into the earth.

Revelation says: "And there was war in heaven"—that is, in the heaven-world, which we call the etheric octave.

Michael and his angels fought against the dragon; and the dragon fought and his angels,

And prevailed not; neither was their place found any more in heaven.

And the great dragon was cast out, that old serpent, called the Devil, and Satan, which deceiveth the whole world: he was cast out into the earth, and his angels were cast out with him.[6]

This tells us something very important: that fallen angels were consigned to the earth in human bodies as a consequence of their attempt to violate the Divine Mother and the Christ Child. Church Fathers have vehemently argued against this interpretation of Revelation. But I tell you that it is so. These fallen angels were literally cast into physical bodies, where they would have to work out their karma and evolve through those physical bodies.

The Christ Child is the real identity of each one on earth. God sent forth that only-begotten Son as the Divine Manchild and he gave to each of us that personal presence of the Christ. There is only one Christ, one Son of God. Each one of us is given that living Christ Presence that we might commune personally with our Lord.

THE GREAT REBELLION *and the* FALLEN ANGELS

Lucifer was an archangel at the time he was cast out of heaven. In the Great Rebellion he caused the fall of many other angels under him. Revelation says that "his tail drew the third part of the stars of heaven, and did cast them to earth."[7] Through their pride and ambition, a third of the angels fell from their state of heavenly grace and followed him. Many among them were required to take embodiment upon earth to work out their karma.

What exactly was Lucifer's sin? He committed the first act of self-idolatry. He fell through pride, ambition and defiance of the laws of God. He talked to God and said, "I can run this universe better than you and certainly better than your Son. I am higher in the order of hierarchy than your Son, and I will not bow down before him. I will not recognize him and I will not serve him." And all of the angels who followed him in that wave of pride said the same.

Saint Francis de Sales recognized the power of Archangel Michael to defeat the rebel angels and the spirit of pride they have attempted to sow in the hearts of God's children. He wrote, "Veneration of St. Michael is the greatest remedy against despising the rights of God, against insubordination, skepticism, and infidelity."[8] Michael gives us the faith to follow the commandments of God, to fortify our willpower and access God's own strength that we might be steadfast on the right course.

THE WAR *on* EARTH

Ever since Michael cast the rebel angels out of heaven, there has been a war on earth. The scripture says: "Woe to the inhabiters of the earth and of the sea! for the devil is come down unto you, having great wrath, because he knoweth that he hath but a short time."[9]

This war is taking place today. Look at our children and youth—some get hooked on drugs or begin having sex at an early age. These behaviors make them susceptible to devastating diseases. Look at what is happening to their bodies, souls and minds. This is the war in the streets of our cities.

We have a big challenge on our hands. Who among us could even begin to consider that we could meet this challenge? Of ourselves we cannot do it, but with God and his angels we can. And if we will learn to talk with the angels, to call them into action, we will see how millions of angels can turn things around.

God gave the fallen angels a certain time to repent of their sin. But they continue their diabolical activities. In the introduction to my book *Fallen Angels and the Origins of Evil*, I tell the story of why Church Fathers suppressed Enoch's teaching that fallen angels could incarnate in human bodies. My book includes the entire text of the Book of Enoch, which describes the deeds of the fallen angels.

The Book of Enoch is a missing link in our understanding of our own scriptures. All we know about Enoch from the Bible is that he was "the seventh from Adam." But Enoch is a major presence in our lives, a real and holy being, a saint in heaven, and he is our father. We can call to him as one of the earthly fathers who have been our progenitors. He knows all about the rebel angels and the origins of evil.

So many souls on earth go the way of the lowest common denominator of what they see on television, in the movies and in society. If we are to save these wonderful souls who do not have leaders or teachers and do not know the way to go, we must take up their cause and by our prayers help protect them against the fallen ones.

The fallen angels were not humbled by the experience of being cast out of heaven into the earth. They have never lost their pride. And they will never accept your victory. There *is* a war going on, and therefore you need Archangel Michael every day.

Know that you can call upon Archangel Michael at any time. By daily giving the decrees that he has given us, you lock right into his presence. Just by calling his name and giving devotion to him, you may feel this mighty archangel's instantaneous presence manifest with you. For he is always ready to help you and to send his legions to help you.

We need the archangels. Without them we are no match for the fallen angels in our midst. Archangel Michael is our defender. He and his legions are like cosmic policemen. In fact, in 1950 Pope Pius XII designated him the patron saint of police officers. Michael is the Prince of the Archangels. All angelic hosts serving us are under his command. He told us, "There are days ... when, for one single one of you, I and my legions, in order to defend you, will slay ten thousand demons."[10]

What a tremendous intercession we have! I know that Archangel Michael and his angels have saved me and my family from serious harm dozens of times, perhaps more. I am sure the same is true for you.

MY EXPERIENCE CALLING *to the* ARCHANGELS

While I was serving my apprenticeship under Mark Prophet many years ago in Washington, D.C., I felt myself suddenly come under the grips of fallen angels. I was in a parking lot. I got out of my car and I stood tall and brave. I said to myself, "It's me or them. So here goes." I knew the prayer "I AM Presence, Thou Art Master." I looked up into the blue sky and with all the power I could muster I shouted this call. I repeated it three times just to be sure.

I AM Presence, Thou Art Master

I AM Presence, Thou art Master,
I AM Presence, clear the way!
Let thy Light and all thy Power
Take possession here this hour!
Charge with Victory's mastery,
Blaze blue lightning, blaze thy substance!
Into this thy form descend,
That Perfection and its Glory
Shall blaze forth and earth transcend!

To my amazement I actually *felt* the devils flee from me, and instantly I felt Archangel Michael's presence over me. Had I not made that decision, I might have allowed myself to come under the influence of those fallen angels, to move among them and go their way.

Every day of our lives there are split seconds when we make decisions. Are we going to indulge that little bit of gossip? Are we going to indulge that criticism of someone else? Are we going to indulge that point of pride? When we make that decision to do so, in that moment we are no longer aligning ourselves with God and his living presence within us. We are aligning ourselves with the forces who have come to defeat us ever so subtly.

As long as we live in the flesh, we are subject to temptation. God has a right to test us and to test our mettle. If we have passed a thousand tests, he will still test us another time. If we think or say to anyone, "I've put that behind me for good," either a devil or an angel of God will come along and test us. So never boast about any accomplishment.

Keep it a secret in your heart.

Be on guard and make the decision to reject the negatives and affirm the positives, to be loving instead of hateful. Make those choices immediately. Archangel Michael is your guard and guardian. And when you make those right decisions and reinforce them with this prayer, the devils will definitely flee—not just from you but from your entire household. They run because they are like coyotes—they are cowards and they travel in packs.

When you give this call you are affirming that God is your only master. You're saying, "I AM Presence, thou art the master of my life, and there is no other master in my life." You are affirming, "Hear, O Israel: The LORD our God is one LORD."[11] Don't allow fear or doubt to be your master. Don't allow self-idolatry to be your master. Don't allow greed, lust, money, possessions or other people to be your master. Don't let anything within or without divide you from your God. For if you do you will, at least for that moment, lose your ability to survive spiritually—in your business, in your work, in your health.

Either God is the God of very gods of your life and there is no other power that can move you, or you acknowledge lesser gods. If you are a house divided, if you allow divisions of any kind in your members, then you are vulnerable to forces that will use and abuse you. Yes, these fallen angels will flatter you, but they will chew you up and spit you out. And you will be vulnerable to the end of this life and in all future lifetimes—until you decide to stand, face and conquer the Adversary of your immortality. So make that decision today.

THE POWER *of the* SPOKEN WORD

When you give the call "I AM Presence, Thou Art Master," a cylinder of blue flame descends around you for your protection. Visualize yourself within a tube of white light (as you see it in the Chart of Your Divine Self, page 9), with violet flame in the center and the added layer of blue-flame protection from Archangel Michael outside the tube of light.

You can also give this call on behalf of others. For example, you might be dealing with a teenager who has a serious problem with cocaine or heroin. In such a case, you're dealing with legions of dark forces who are working against the child. That is why addictions are so hard to break—you are not just wrestling against the habit, the substance and its toxicity; you're wrestling against unseen forces.

So you have to be more determined. When you are dealing with possessing demons, you must call upon the LORD to embolden you. This is not the time for meekness. Command the light to act. Command the archangels and their legions to bind these forces. Give the mantra day by day until the action you have called for is accomplished.

God gave you a voice and the power of speech and a throat chakra so that you could deliver the power of his *spoken* Word. If you are not familiar with this dynamic form of prayer, give it a try, especially if nothing else has worked. You just might save a loved one.

To repeat a mantra again and again is also very important. The angels need the momentum of your energy and calls here below to do their job. This is not the vain repetition of prayers. This is a very conscious determination to pray and to "pray without ceasing,"[12] as the Bible says, so that you can be that reinforcing presence side by side with a teenager who is wrestling literally with the very forces of hell.

The religions of the world in all ages, back to Atlantis and Lemuria, have practiced the science of the spoken Word, repeating mantras by the hour to draw down the light of God from the level of the I AM Presence. We live in a dense world, and God lives in the exalted plane of light. To pull that light down, we use his name "I AM" in decrees and prayers so that light gets anchored in our chakras, the vessels that contain the light.

BUILD *a* DAILY MOMENTUM *of* PRAYER

One of the saints of heaven, whose name is Liberty, told us, "Archangel Michael is at your side and does answer your call and does answer it best when you keep a daily momentum"[13] of prayers to him. Your call for help will be answered instantaneously when you have built this momentum.

When you begin to use the prayers to Archangel Michael and repeat them, you come to the place where something changes, something locks in. You feel a whoosh of light and a sensation in your whole body, and you recognize that in that moment your prayers have built a momentum of devotion and have opened the way for Michael to literally descend into your temple and place his presence over you.

It is the most comforting, reassuring feeling to know that God has sent the archangels to so tenderly, so honestly and with such great trust answer the call of every little child and every person on earth. Building a momentum of prayer at the same time every day gives you a reservoir of light sealed in your heart that is available when you come upon difficult situations.

KELLY'S CALL *to* ARCHANGEL MICHAEL

I once received a letter from a woman witnessing to the remarkable intercession of Archangel Michael in the life of her teenage daughter, Kelly.

A few days after Kelly and her friends learned about Archangel Michael, they were in a terrible collision. A fully loaded 18-wheel truck hit their car broadside, rolled up over the car and dragged the car under its wheels for five hundred feet before stopping. Kelly was pinned in the crushed metal from the bottom of her feet to mid-chest. One wheel of the truck was directly above her lower body and she was not able to breathe. With all the strength Kelly had left, in the silence of her heart she called to Archangel Michael for help.

Instantly the truck lifted. She had time to twist the upper part of her little body free. Then the weight of the truck descended again. Kelly received a crushed pelvis, her leg was snapped in half and she had internal injuries. She was in extreme pain but she could breathe and she was alive! Through the grace of God, Archangel Michael heard her silent call and came as he had promised.

Those who witnessed this event could not explain what happened. They only knew that a miracle had taken place and that a life had been spared. Through the grace of God and after three surgeries, Kelly's body was repaired. Kelly's mother concluded her letter: "I witness to you that Archangel Michael is always at our side. He simply wants our call, and he may not intercede unless he is asked."

NOTHING IS HOPELESS—MAKE *the* CALL!

Sometimes when you assess a situation, you think it's so hopeless that not even the archangels can do anything about it. Well, that is just when you need to give the calls, when you have to remember that there is always a little devil here or there to whisper in your ear and tell you that the archangels cannot help you. Or maybe you plan to make the calls after you finish this project, and the project winds up being six hours long and you forget to make the call.

Surrender the situation to the will of God. Sometimes people are rescued from death, and sometimes they are not. We are not God and we should not play God. We do not hold the fate of men and nations in our hands, nor do we pretend to know the course of people's karma or the will of God for them. But one thing is certain: Our call *will* compel the answer —God's answer for that person and the maximum amount of mercy that the Law will afford that person and that situation.

The angels tell us: "Just make the call. If you don't make the call, for sure we can't help you." But if you do, "having faith as a grain of mustard seed," the Great Law itself will see to it that all that can be done for the one or the many who are in distress will be done.

More than that we cannot expect, for God does not break his laws. He does not break the law of karma, and we all have karma to deal with. Sometimes when we go through a little pain and injury it softens our heart. We become more humble, we learn profound lessons about life, we become more grateful and perhaps not so proud anymore. God is teaching us in many ways. We can be grateful for every trial.

ARCHANGEL MICHAEL'S ANGELS
ASSIST US PERSONALLY

Archangel Michael has assigned members of his legions to assist us personally. The archangels actually assign to us angels as though they were our personal staff. You can assign your angels to prepare the way for successful meetings, to work out impossible problems. You can command them to undertake special projects on behalf of your family, your business, your church. You can ask them to tutor your children as they do their homework, to help them with a learning problem, to help you establish meaningful relationships with the right people. You can ask for their help with mundane as well as spiritual things.

Someone wrote me this story of how Archangel Michael helped her. She had been visiting her parents in wintertime in New England. It had just snowed, and her father had gotten a rented van stuck in the driveway. He tried rocking it to no avail. Then he pushed, with the girl at the wheel. Then they both pushed, but still no luck. The more they pushed, the deeper the van got stuck.

After half an hour or so, the daughter, who was only five foot three, convinced her father to get back into the van and start rocking again while *she* pushed by herself. *Then* she made an intense call to Archangel Michael to place his presence over her and to *push that van*.

In under one minute, the van was out of the rut and onto the road. The father was dumbfounded. How could his tiny daughter have been able to move the van by herself? She told him she had not moved the van at all—it was Archangel Michael.

ARCHANGEL MICHAEL'S COMMITMENT *to* YOU

Archangel Michael made the commitment to every one of us that if we would give our decrees to him for twenty minutes each day, he would assign an angel to be with us until the hour of our victory. Twenty minutes of decrees is not hard to do, especially while you're driving here and there.

I would like to share with you a story of how one diligent decreer turned the tide by invoking the power of Archangel Michael. For seven months in 1985 a serial killer called the "Night Stalker" committed fourteen murders and twenty rapes and assaults in Los Angeles and San Francisco. He entered the homes of his victims at night through unlocked doors and windows.

On August 31, the woman who told me this story got up at 5 a.m. Something came over her and she felt in her heart the intense determination that this was the day the "Night Stalker" had to be caught. She started by giving a rosary to Archangel Michael.[14] She repeated it by the hour, dedicating it to one purpose—the catching of the "Night Stalker."

That very day Richard Ramirez was caught in an East Los Angeles neighborhood when residents saw him trying to steal a car. They captured him and held him until the police arrived. Police determined that Ramirez's fingerprints matched those found in a stolen car known to have been used by the "Night Stalker."

You may not believe that this was accomplished through the action of one individual who decided to keep a vigil because Archangel Michael communicated to her that this was the moment when this man could be taken. They say miracles are for believers. And you yourself will become a believer when you start realizing the many miracles this archangel will perform both *for* you and *through* you in your prayers for others.

It only takes one person with determination to turn the tide of something that is very dark and malignant. Many people may have been praying about this situation. What this person did that was different is that she concentrated her calls to Archangel Michael, determined in her heart this was the day, and she did not leave her prayer vigil until what she intended was accomplished.

If you think you are facing a problem that simply cannot be resolved, I counsel you to go to Archangel Michael and prove him. No matter how big the problem seems in your own life or even on a national scale, turn to Archangel Michael.

PUT *on the* WHOLE ARMOUR *of* GOD

Archangel Michael says that in addition to calling to his angels to intercede, you may join his legions in their service to the earth for three hours on each night that you volunteer. When you retire at night, call to him to come and take you, to clothe you with the armour of the angels so that you can join his legions and learn how to go into battle with them for the protection of souls of light.

Michael also invites you to join in his councils in his retreat at Banff and have a say as to where you would direct his legions. Call to him to take your soul to his retreat while your body sleeps. His angels will recharge your soul with their tremendous energy and light.

As Archangel Michael's angels never go to battle without their armour of light and the full protection of the Law, Michael charges us to do likewise: to put on the whole armour of God. He dictated this direction to the apostle Paul, and Paul wrote it in his epistle to the Ephesians. This is what Archangel Michael told him:

Put on the whole armour of God, that ye may be able to stand against the wiles of the devil....
Stand therefore, having your loins girt about with truth, and having on the breastplate of righteousness;
And your feet shod with the preparation of the gospel of peace;
Above all, taking the shield of faith, wherewith ye shall be able to quench all the fiery darts of the wicked.
And take the helmet of salvation, and the sword of the Spirit, which is the word of God.[15]

This command tells us that righteousness and honor and the virtues of God are our real protection. Archangel Michael says that in answer to your call he will give you his armour and shield. As you work daily to remove your weaknesses, this armour will be strengthened.

ARCHANGEL MICHAEL BRINGS *the* GIFT *of* FAITH

The gift of faith is a very great gift. And that is the gift that Archangel Michael brings to you. Many people doubt. They doubt themselves, they doubt God, they have a great deal of fear, and they fear God. Faith is not an active element in their lives, and yet we all need to have faith in something. People will fail us from time to time, but God will not fail us and the angels will not fail us.

As you pray and decree with absolute faith in God and in the power of his spoken Word through you, what you are calling for will manifest—unless what you are decreeing for is not the will of God or the timing is not right for the answer to your prayer to be made manifest.

Doubt blocks the physical manifestation of your decrees. Archangel Michael has said that if we give him our doubts and fears, he will give back to us his full momentum of faith and his devotion to the will of God. He strengthened Joan of Arc to go forward when all seemed lost. He whispered in her ear, "Charge! Charge! Charge!" She repeated the command and galvanized the forces of France to fight in defense of liberty.

My prayer for each and every one of you is that you become the friend of Archangel Michael so that when you have need of a friend he will be there.

MICHAEL *and* FAITH

RAY AND COLOR	*First ray, blue*
QUALITIES	*God-power, perfection and protection, God's will*
CHAKRA	*Throat — 16 petals*
PROMINENT ON	*Tuesday*
SPIRITUAL RETREAT	*Over Banff, Canada*

ASK THEM FOR:

SPIRITUAL GIFTS	*Faith, perfecting of your soul, your divine blueprint, freedom from fear and doubt*
PERSONAL ASSISTANCE WITH	*Physical and spiritual protection and safety at home, away and when traveling; binding of psychic aggressors and evil spirits*
HELP WITH WORLD ISSUES	*Inspiration for leaders, improvement of government*

COMMUNING *with* ANGELS *of* FAITH *and* PROTECTION

MAKE THE CALL

Just as Archangel Michael strengthened Joan of Arc, he will also strengthen you in your hour of need. He says that when everything seems to be going wrong, you can call to his legions with the command: "Charge! Charge! Charge! and let victory be proclaimed!"

Charge! Charge! Charge! and let victory be proclaimed!
Charge! Charge! Charge! and let victory be proclaimed!
Charge! Charge! Charge! and let victory be proclaimed!

Give that call with the full power of your being, and accept nothing less than victory every day of your life.

USE THE NAME OF GOD

When you talk to God, say your prayers and decrees aloud and speak with authority. You can command the angels to take action if you do so in the name of God, I AM THAT I AM. Our lesser self has no authority to command God or his angels, but as scripture says, "Whosoever will call upon the name of the LORD will be saved."[16]

So, to begin a decree or mantra, you can say, "In the name of God, I AM THAT I AM, in the name of my Mighty I AM Presence and Christ Self, [then add the names of the legions of light whose action you are invoking, for example, "in the name of Archangel Michael"], I decree." Then give the decree. Here is one to Archangel Michael:

Traveling Protection

Lord Michael before, Lord Michael behind,
Lord Michael to the right, Lord Michael to the left,
Lord Michael above, Lord Michael below,
Lord Michael, Lord Michael wherever I go!

I AM his love protecting here!
I AM his love protecting here!
I AM his love protecting here! (repeat 3 or 9 times)

As you repeat this decree, visualize Archangel Michael coming to you in full armour with a mighty sword of blue flame, cutting you free from everything that is not of God, that is not of the light.

You can give "Traveling Protection" anytime, anywhere—even if you are staying at home. See Michael before you, behind you, to your right, to your left, above you, beneath you, and in the center of your form. Everywhere you go, there is Archangel Michael.

When you are driving your car to work, call for Archangel Michael to be around your car and around every other car on that highway—and on every highway or road in the entire world. It takes no more time to multiply your call, to give that prayer for every person who is traveling on any form of transportation anywhere. Archangel Michael can duplicate his manifestation a billion times and still have the full presence of his being wherever he is called.

CALL FOR THE ARMOUR OF GOD

One way to invoke the armour of God is to call forth your tube of light. As you give this decree, visualize yourself standing in the violet flame, surrounded by the tube of dazzling white light from your Mighty I AM Presence (see Chart on page 9). See it coalesce around you as intense white fire, a cylinder of absolute protection from the heart of God.

Tube of Light

Beloved I AM Presence bright,
Round me seal your tube of light
From ascended master flame
Called forth now in God's own name.
Let it keep my temple free
From all discord sent to me.

I AM calling forth violet fire
To blaze and transmute all desire,
Keeping on in freedom's name
Till I AM one with the violet flame. (repeat 3 times)

How Angels Help You
Contact Your Higher Self

3

ARCHANGEL JOPHIEL *and* CHRISTINE

*A*ngels are all around us. But sometimes their presence, their vibration, and our ability to feel them and to contact them is drowned out by the noise all around us. Even when we don't hear the sounds of modern life, we may feel the energies bombarding our senses.

It takes time apart and a special place to enter into daily meditation and to build a momentum of meditation, especially if we desire direct communion with the mind of God and the angels who facilitate that communion. The angel to call to specifically for the mind of God and the opening of the crown chakra is Archangel Jophiel, for he brings the wisdom of God, illumination, understanding, and gnosis (your self-knowledge in God).

Jophiel and Christine are the archangel and archeia of the second ray, the ray of God's wisdom. They come to banish ignorance and to bring enlightenment. Angels of the second ray quicken your capacity to attune with the universal mind of God. They work with you through the crown chakra, known in the East as the thousand-petaled lotus. It is golden yellow in color, and you can visualize it right at the crown of your head.

The crown chakra has 972 petals, each of which carries its own specific frequency or vibration for the quickening of our minds. There is but one universal mind of God, and we all tie into that one Mind. When we clear our brain and unburden it of dense foods and substances that cloud our mind, our brain can be the vessel for the mind of God.

The opening of the mind of God in you comes through meditation upon the crown chakra and through embodying the flame of wisdom. When you are contacting the light, you might feel a vibration or tingling of your crown chakra as the light enters the brain and travels to that chakra. Some hear it in their ear as the sound of a waterfall.

The name Jophiel means "beauty of God." Some traditions say that Jophiel is the guardian of the Tree of the Knowledge of Good and Evil. He is the protector of earnest seekers of truth and is said to have been the teacher of the sons of Noah. In some traditions Jophiel is considered the prince of the Law (or Torah) and the archangel who instructed Moses in the mystery of the Kabbalah. He is the archangel who sponsors the wisdom teachings of Gautama Buddha, Confucius and Lao Tze. He also ministers to the Lord Christ and his disciples.

Jophiel and Christine's mission is to deliver us from profound levels of ignorance that are settling over every nation, starting with the earliest grades of school. Call to them and their angels to unveil the mysteries of God and expose the infamies of men and fallen angels. They reveal what is hidden in government, science, education, medicine, food, the environment, the war on drugs, the effects of music on evolution, and in all things that touch our daily lives.

The retreat of Jophiel and Christine is south of the Great Wall near Lanchow, north-central China. Isn't it interesting that we associate the great wisdom of the ancients with the Chinese?

ARCHANGELS APPEAR *to the* APOSTLES

In the Book of Acts, an angel appeared to Cornelius, a Roman centurion and gentile, and told him to send men to Joppa to find the apostle Peter. The angel gave Cornelius the exact location where the men could find Peter—and following the angel's instructions, they did. Acts also records that an angel released Peter from prison.

The apostle Paul encountered an angel when he was on board a ship that was in danger of sinking. The angel told Paul that he was destined to appear before Caesar, and for this reason God had granted the safety of all who were sailing with him. Paul later told those on board, "I ask you not to give way to despair. There will be no loss of life at all, only of the ship. Last night there appeared beside me an angel of ... God."[1]

The angels who rescued Peter and Paul were archangels. The apostles were people just like us and they had encounters with angels. So expect your own encounters with angels.

ARCHANGELS ARE ANCIENT BEINGS

Archangels are so ancient that they antedate the creation of worlds. They are the very first beings that God created. Whether we talk about an archangel as he is today or as he was a hundred thousand years ago, he is the same being. While we come and go lifetime after lifetime, the archangels and their legions of light have been forever in the being of God.

Archangel Jophiel has said that at times his angels form a

column of light from here to the Great Central Sun, which is beyond what is known or visible to us. You can imagine Jophiel and Christine and their legions wearing golden robes, their fiery brilliance almost blinding. These angels occupy the golden-yellow sphere surrounding the white-fire center of the Great Central Sun. They appear as shafts of yellow fire from the Sun, and that dazzling brilliance hints at the power they have to quicken our minds.

ANGELS TEACH YOU DAILY

Jophiel and Christine are teachers of mankind. Their legions of angels are teaching you every day, inspiring you. Their thoughts so easily enter your mind that in one moment you didn't have an idea in your mind about how you were going to do something, and in the next moment you have the idea, the plan, the blueprint.

The brain is a magnificent instrument. I see it as a chalice. The central nervous system, subconscious and unconscious minds, and chakras are all chalices, receptors of the intelligence of the mind of God. We get ideas that set us sailing in our careers and enable us to be successful. How many of those ideas originate in the human brain? And how many of them really come from the Higher Mind, from the God Presence, from the universal intelligence? I am continuously humbled before the intimations of God that I and others receive that simply could not have come forth from ourselves but are truly a gift.

When you work with the angels of the second ray, you are working to become totally bonded to your Higher Self so that the Christ Presence (see the Chart on page 9) is no longer above you but fully integrated with you here below. That is the nature of the great avatars of all ages. Jesus Christ was fully the manifestation, the incarnation of the Son of God. He set the example and the pattern of what all can do.

EXPAND YOUR MENTAL CAPACITY

Archeia Christine says you are absolutely not limited to what is considered the norm of mental capacity. She says you've been brainwashed to believe that only a privileged few can have a superior intellect. What a tragedy, she says, that people limit children's mental capacity by an IQ test. Because people accept that as a limit to brain development, the angels of illumination cannot infire their minds with the capacity of the Higher Mind. Although brain matter responds, the human consciousness in its sense of limitation does not.

When this happens, Christine says, the human consciousness is not an open door and so does not receive the infiring. She says people use only one-tenth of their mental capacity, but this will change when you call to the angels of wisdom and enlightenment to help the entire population of earth to come up into their own higher consciousness.

Christine says that illumination's golden flame has the power to mold your brain—to raise you to a level where you are using 20, 30, 40, 50 percent of your capacity and finally 100 percent of the raw material you had when you were born. Think of that!

ACCESS *the* CHRIST MIND *and* YOUR HIGHER SELF

Quickening our capacity to attune with the universal mind of God is what we are about. At your signal, the angels of wisdom are ready and waiting to help you absorb elements of the mind of God. Archangel Jophiel remarked, "Do you know that a single mind, transformed by the mind of Christ, is a catalyst for quickening the minds of the population of an entire planet?"[2] That is what the Christ incarnate, the Buddha incarnate can do.

Paul said, "Let this mind be in you which was also in Christ Jesus."[3] Paul himself witnessed the mind of Jesus Christ one with the mind of God. Many Christians believe they cannot be like Jesus, who was and is the greatest rabbi who ever lived. But Jesus is telling you today that you *can* have the mind of Christ, the mind of Buddha, the mind of God. He guarantees that you can have that mind. But if you don't believe it, if you have accepted the lie of Satan that you are a condemned sinner and have no right to walk and talk with Jesus as your friend and brother and rabbi, then your own self-appraisal will deprive you of the ownership of that mind.

As Jesus said two thousand years ago, so he says today: "Everything I have done, you can do, and more, because through your Holy Christ Self you have the same connection to God that I do." This is what Jesus said that is recorded in scripture: "He that believeth on me, the works that I do shall he do also; and greater works than these shall he do; because I go unto my Father."[4]

Jophiel says that if you want to be in control of your life, then you must have access to the Christ mind. In a dictation he advised us:

Pursue the path of the imitation of Christ. Speak as you know or believe Christ would speak—with love but firmness, sternness where required, mercy when it is due, soft-spoken when needed, in the intensity of the sacred fire when you would awake a soul who does not want to be awakened. Speak as Christ would speak and Christ will speak through you. Think as Christ would think and Christ will think through you and the mind of God will become congruent with the physical vessel. And there shall be no separation, as things equal to the same things are equal to each other—one Christ, one Lord, one manifestation in your temple![5]

When you hear yourself saying things you know Jesus would not say, in that moment you are far from your Holy Christ Self as well as from Jesus Christ. The Christ Presence separates itself from human discord and rises to heavenly octaves of spiritual harmony.

By a pure and penitent heart, through prayer and violet-flame decrees you can reestablish your harmony with the flame of forgiveness and loving-kindness which you share with all. When you do that, the Christ Presence draws nigh to you again.

Don't condemn yourself when you make a mistake or become angry, for by that vibration you are still pushing away the Christ Presence. There is nothing productive about self-condemnation. If you make a mistake, pick yourself up, acknowledge that you erred, then do whatever is necessary to correct the wrong and get on with your life.

The fallen angels plague us with self-condemnation, sometimes all the days of our lives. Authoritarian parents may have indoctrinated us with an absence of self-worth whereby we condemn ourselves. We need to get beyond those feelings, because God is real in us.

Angels and masters gravitate to higher realms, so to be with them and commune with them you must raise your consciousness. This is the law of octaves. You can accelerate your consciousness through your prayers and meditation and by your love, harmony, peace and understanding. This is the key to making contact with them and with your Higher Self. By the same process, you can draw your Higher Self, the angels and ascended masters down to your level once you have reconsecrated your heart and soul and aura by your devotions.

ANGELS DISPEL IGNORANCE

The angels of the second ray of wisdom and enlightenment have the job to rescue the souls of the world from ignorance—ignorance of the laws of God, ignorance of their own true identity in God. The sages of East and West define ignorance as blindness to the true nature of the Real Self.

Gautama Buddha taught that ignorance of one's true nature causes inordinate desire, which is the basis of all suffering and the reason why we keep reincarnating. The texts of Hinduism teach that ignorance is the origin of pain and that pain will not cease until ignorance is entirely dispelled. So if that is true, we will not know when ignorance is entirely dispelled except from the standpoint of our own enlightenment.

Each day is a proving of what really is the wisdom of God and what is the education of man. We never know just how ignorant we were until we gain just a bit more enlightenment. Then, when we get to the next level and we look back, we see that we were not too bright even then.

EDUCATE *the* HEART, MIND *and* SOUL

Jophiel and Christine are concerned about the deplorable state of education. Their angels wage relentless warfare against ignorance, mental density and mediocrity, as these affect the minds of educators and students and lower the standards of institutions of learning. Jophiel says these negative attitudes "detract from the crispness of the Christ qualities that belong to and are the inheritance of the children of the Sun."[6]

Jophiel says that we need to educate the heart, then the mind and then the soul. He says: "Think of the ancients who walked the earth and knew the thoughts of God when God thought them."[7]

In our time, the goal of education on earth has been to accelerate the computer of the mental body. Direct communication with God through the heart is wanting. Without the discriminating intelligence of the Higher Self, man is little more than a computer, a flesh-and-body machine. That's why from the hour of conception parents must begin and continue the ritual of the education of the heart, the mind and the soul. Then man will realize his potential to become a son of God.

Archeia Christine asks us to call to her to intercede to release advanced teaching methods to the parents, teachers and sponsors of youth. She says:

Will you not pray that the World Teachers and the hierarchies of illumination might release to instructors in every field, as well as to yourselves, new and advanced methods of teaching all subjects. We have released methods through Maria Montessori and many other educators. There is so much more that we can deliver to those who will listen.[8]

DON'T UNDERESTIMATE WHAT
the ANGELS CAN DO *for* YOU

Jophiel and Christine teach you to call upon their untold legions of angels to help you with the most minute details of your personal life, even as you call upon them in matters of national or international crisis. We tend to underestimate what the angels can and will do for us, so just give it a try. Prove that what I am saying is true.

One of my students had this experience:

One time I needed to get permission from a company to use a passage from one of their publications, and this was a rush project. My memo was brief and included the standard wording for these kinds of requests, but I was asking permission for not only current use but also a variety of possible future uses. I remember thinking, "It sure feels like a wish list."

As the fax machine was sending my memo, I made a heartfelt call to Archangel Jophiel. It was the first time I had made a specific call to him. I put the entire matter in his hands.

Usually it takes days or weeks to receive a response to these kinds of requests. But sitting in the tray of the fax machine less than an hour later was a reply. "That was amazingly fast," I thought. "I hope it's good news." As I read the fax, I saw that they had graciously responded, granted all my requests without any restrictions—and didn't charge a fee! I praised Archangel Jophiel for his wonderful intercession. I knew we should expect answers to our prayers, but I'm still in awe at the swiftness of his response.

Another student told me this story:

When I was driving home with some fellow students, my car developed a problem and began to seriously overheat. None of us had any more money to spare and we were going home "on a wing and a prayer"—literally.

Each time the needle started creeping up hotter and hotter, I would make intense calls to the angels and nature spirits. I told the people in the car to hold the visualization and thoughtform of snow, of crystal clear, cold mountain streams and ice all around the whole engine. Then we would watch the needle immediately go right back down as the temperature dropped to normal. It was such a wonderful testimony to the power of the Word and the intercession of heavenly helpers.

Remember to use visualization. Whatever the problem is, put all of your attention into that thoughtform as you give your calls for assistance.

THE ARCHANGELS RESPECT FREE WILL

When you call to the archangels in the name of God, I AM THAT I AM, and in the name of Jesus Christ or your Christ Self, they are bound by cosmic law to help you—as long as your requests are in keeping with the will of God, and as long as you submit to that will. Their answer, though, is not always obvious, and it is often in roundabout ways that we find the answer coming together in our lives.

This is an example of a prayer that you can make to the archangels:

In the name I AM THAT I AM, in the name of Jesus Christ, beloved Archangel Jophiel and Christine, I ask you to lock the mind of God over every man, woman and child on this planet that we might see and know and be the living Truth, that our leaders might give us true leadership and that they might reach the right resolution of all problems facing the governments of the nations. Archangel Jophiel and Christine, I call to you and I accept it done right now in full power in answer to my call.

When you make a call like that to Jophiel and Christine, accept that they have answered you instantaneously. In this case I accept that they have locked the mind of God over every single person on earth. Now comes free will. Some people will accept that mind. Some will be healed by it. Some will reject it, either consciously or unconsciously.

Why don't the angels help us without our prayers and directions to them? The crux of the matter is that we exercised free will and left the realms of perfection. We said to God, "We are not content to abide by your will. We are going to go through a period of experimentation, exercising the free will that you gave us in the beginning." This experiment has turned out to last many thousands of years.

God gave us this physical universe, this planetary home and other planetary homes for us to try our hand at free will. He made a pact with us and he said: "You are now living in the footstool kingdom. It is your kingdom. You have chosen to run it. And so our angels will not interfere with your free will unless you ask them to, unless you come to the place where you accept and call for the will of God."

This is the reason why angels don't just take care of everything, why they don't prevent every accident, every calamity, every war, every fire that happens, every death of a child.

"Why doesn't God just stop it all? Why does he let all these things happen?" A lot of people use that logic as a rationale for being perpetually angry with God. They don't understand that we are all reaping our karma. And they don't understand that we have opted for freedom.

Many people fear the will of God because it could change their whole life, and they are pretty comfortable where they are right now. But God doesn't want us to be robots under his control. He endowed us with his flame, his divine spark. He gave us our I AM Presence to be with us at all times, and he gave us a Christ Presence or Buddhic Presence. He gave us all these things on the basis of free will. We even have the free will to snuff out that flame in our heart by a deep anger against God.

We have bungled around so long that some of us have concluded it is just no use continuing our own way, with our own free will, because sooner or later things just do not go as they should. If you get to that point, you might decide to try God's will and to call for that will in your life daily. Offer a prayer to God that you will go wherever his will takes you and that you will maintain a listening ear to obey the inner voice of God. That is a wonderful relationship to have with God.

JOPHIEL *and* CHRISTINE

RAY AND COLOR	*Second ray, golden yellow*
QUALITIES	*Wisdom, illumination and enlightenment*
CHAKRA	*Crown – 972 petals*
PROMINENT ON	*Sunday*
SPIRITUAL RETREAT	*Near Lanchow, north central China*

ASK THEM FOR:

SPIRITUAL GIFTS	*Wisdom, illumination, understanding, inspiration, knowledge, connection with your Higher Self*
PERSONAL ASSISTANCE WITH	*Absorbing and retaining information, studying, passing tests; freedom from addictions; mental health; open-mindedness*
HELP WITH WORLD ISSUES	*Enlightenment for leaders in government, business, education and religion; cleaning up our planet; reform of education*

COMMUNING *with* ANGELS *of* WISDOM

CONTACTING YOUR HIGHER SELF

Ask Jophiel and Christine and the angels of wisdom to help you contact your Higher Self. You don't need a long or formal prayer. You can simply say:

Beloved Archangel Jophiel and Christine and legions of light, come to me now. Help me. Help my soul to make contact with my Higher Self. I want to commune with that part of me. I want to become my Higher Self here on earth. I want to be able to do those greater things that Jesus promised me I would do because he is in the heart of the Father.

O Jophiel and Christine, correct me, show me what is acceptable and not acceptable in the sight of God. Teach me the way. I am but a child. I would learn. I would listen. Come into my house. Help my children. Help my marriage. Help my family. Help me to find the job I need to support myself and those who depend on me.

Talk to them about whether you need to go back to school, get a degree, study at new levels so you can help more people. Talk to them about your divine plan and ask for assistance with it. Talk to them as if they were standing two feet in front of you. They hear every word. God created them aeons ago so that when you wanted help to find your path, Jophiel and Christine and their legions would be here for you.

Talk to God and his angels with a prayer from your heart, with your heart on fire with the love you have for them and on fire with the desire to truly walk in the shadow of the Almighty.

CROWN CHAKRA MEDITATION

When you engage in a chakra meditation, place your left hand over your heart and your right hand on the chakra you wish to activate. You are making contact with your I AM Presence when you do this. To activate the crown, place the thumb and first two fingers of your right hand at the crown of your head. Visualize a bright yellow flame leaping and pulsating from that point. Your left hand is taking the fire of your heart and your right hand is using that fire to quicken the crown chakra. Then speak to the flame, the extension of God's presence:

O flame of light bright and gold,
O flame most wondrous to behold,
I AM in every brain cell shining,
I AM in light's wisdom all divining.
Ceaseless, flowing fount of illumination flaming,
I AM, I AM, I AM illumination.

Repeat this as many times as you wish, speaking it with all the joy of your heart, the expectancy, the absolute conviction that Jophiel is establishing this flame in your crown chakra.

The angels will help you contact your Higher Self through mantra. As you meditate on the angels, pour your love and devotion to them and exercise the power of speech to affirm God where you are. You are coming into consonance with your Real Self, the Holy Christ Self, when you do this.

When you put all of these things together and establish a

pattern of communion with God, your aura will change. Not only will your own Christ Presence drop over you by increments, but the angels will also come and magnify your aura for the work that you have to do each day. They are your very willing helpers.

SALUTATION TO THE SUN

This mantra is a perfect way to start a daily yoga or meditation session or any physical exercise. Beginning with this salutation to the sun, you consecrate your physical body, your desire body, your mental body, your memory body to God.

O mighty Presence of God, I AM, in and behind the Sun:
I welcome thy light, which floods all the earth,
    into my life, into my mind, into my spirit, into my soul.
Radiate and blaze forth thy light!
Break the bonds of darkness and superstition!
Charge me with the great clearness
    of thy white fire radiance!
I AM thy child, and each day I shall become
    more of thy manifestation!

When you see the words *I AM* in these prayers and mantras, remember that this is the name God gave to Moses. When you affirm "I AM," you are really saying, "The I AM THAT I AM who is my Real Self is," and then you name the action or quality. In this way you are drawing the light of God to bring into manifestation what you have named.

How Angels Help You
Experience More Love

4

CHARITY

CHAPTER 4

ARCHANGEL CHAMUEL *and* CHARITY

*D*ivine love is the most opposed force on the planet. The fallen angels are determined to take from you the divine love that you can express to one another and to all whom you meet. Why? When you have love in your heart, the angels will multiply your love many times over, and your love then becomes the abiding place for the living Christ to reach out to all whom you meet.

Jesus said: "A new commandment I give unto you, That ye love one another; as I have loved you, that ye also love one another. By this shall all men know that ye are my disciples."[1] And so, to secure your discipleship under the living Christ, your Holy Christ Self, and to make your heart his abode, you must be strong in your conviction to affirm love every day and not let anything take from you the love of God. For, as the apostle Paul said, "all the law is fulfilled in one word, even in this; Thou shalt love thy neighbour as thyself."[2]

Chamuel and Charity are the archangels who teach us to develop the qualities of mercy and compassion, loving care and concern for others. The work of these archangels and their legions corresponds to the heart chakra, representing God's love, creativity and beauty. They serve on the third ray, the ray of divine love. The color of this ray ranges from pink to rose to ruby.

The name Chamuel means "he who sees God." When we have love in our hearts we can also see God. Chamuel and Charity are mentioned in various traditions. Some sources say Chamuel was the angel who wrestled with Jacob and who strengthened Jesus in the Garden of Gethsemane.

ARCHEIA CHARITY

Archeia Charity is the twin flame of Archangel Chamuel. She has worked for centuries to help earth's children balance their karma through service to life. She tutored the ascended lady master Nada, a magnificent spiritual being, in Nada's final embodiment on earth.

Nada was the youngest child in a large, exceptionally gifted family. Charity appeared to her at a young age and taught her how to draw God's love from her heart and radiate it into the nature kingdom for the blessing of life. Charity taught Nada to expand the flame in her heart so that she might be instrumental in the quickening of her brothers' and sisters' chakras.

Nada supported her siblings while they achieved standing in their respective professions. Her inner spiritual work was to tend the flame on the altar of their hearts while they used their energies and talents to make major contributions to their culture.

Nada explained that to all outer appearances she had not accomplished much. Her joy and eternal reward came in nourishing the hearts of her family so that they might succeed and in knowing that her service had been essential to their victory. She sacrificed what might have been a brilliant career of her own and made her ascension at the conclusion of that lifetime of surrender to love and selfless service.

THE CHERUBIM

Among the numberless numbers of angels who serve with Chamuel and Charity on the third ray of divine love are the covering cherubim. The word *cherubim* (the Hebrew plural of *cherub*) comes from an Akkadian word meaning "one who prays" or "one who intercedes" or from the Assyrian word meaning "to be near." Thus, *cherubim* means near ones, attendants, or bodyguards. In rabbinic tradition, cherubim are the throne-bearers and charioteers of God. Their role is to guard the holiness of God.

Islam teaches that the cherubim chant continually "Glory to Allah" and dwell where the devil cannot attack them. In Christianity, the cherubim are considered to be among the highest orders of angels.

The cherubim are the first angels mentioned in the Old Testament. Genesis says that after the LORD God expelled Adam and Eve from Paradise, "He placed at the east of the garden of Eden Cherubims, and a flaming sword which turned every way, to keep the way of the tree of life."[3]

The Old Testament records that the cherubim bear God's throne in the Holy of holies, the innermost sanctuary of the temple, and describes the LORD as dwelling between the cherubim. The LORD instructed Moses that in building the tabernacle he should place a gold cherub on each side of the mercy seat, which is the lid of the Ark of the Covenant.

The LORD said to Moses:

The cherubims shall stretch forth their wings on high, covering the mercy seat with their wings, and their faces shall look one to another....

And thou shalt put the mercy seat above upon the ark. And in the ark thou shalt put the testimony that I shall give thee.

And there I will meet with thee, and from above the mercy seat, from between the two cherubims which are upon the ark of the testimony, I will speak with thee of all things which I will give thee in commandment unto the children of Israel.[4]

One commentator writes:

According to the old rabbis, the name of the one [cherub on the mercy seat] was Righteousness and of the other Mercy; but some ancient interpreters have said that while usually their faces were half turned away from each other, yet when peace and righteousness ruled among the people they turned toward each other, and bending forward kissed each other.[5]

In Solomon's Temple in Jerusalem, the walls were covered with carvings of cherubim. The Book of Ezekiel records Ezekiel's vision of four cherubim:

And I looked and, behold, a whirlwind came out of the north, a great cloud, and a fire infolding itself, and a brightness was about it; and out of the midst thereof the color of amber, out of the midst of the fire. Also out of the midst thereof came the likeness of four living creatures. And this was their appearance: they had the likeness of a man.

Ezekiel described each cherub as having four faces, four wings, and hooves like those of a calf. He said:

As for the likeness of the living creatures, their appearance was like burning coals of fire, and like the appearance of lamps; it went up and down among the living creatures; and the fire was bright, and out of the fire went forth lightning.[6]

Until the eleventh century, cherubim were depicted with mature faces framed by two to six large wings. This image was meant to convey the pure spirit, intelligence and swiftness of the cherubim. In later religious art, the cherubim were standardly depicted with plump infant heads and curly hair framed by a cluster of small wings. Thus was lost the original understanding of cherubim as the powerful, fiery guardians of the covenants God made with his people through Moses.

Archeia Charity promises that two angels of the legions of Chamuel and Charity will stand by you until the hour of your ascension as long as you walk the path of divine love. These angels are understudies of the cherubim. They will serve as guardians to protect you against malice, slander, and all misunderstandings directed against you. Their joy and their reason for being is to adore the flame that burns in your heart. Charity says the devotion of these angels will increase the aura of pink light surrounding your heart chakra.

THE RETREAT *of* CHAMUEL *and* CHARITY

Archangel Chamuel and Charity welcome us to study in their etheric retreat in the heaven-world over Saint Louis. Gateway Arch, on the bank of the Mississippi River, communicates to the soul at inner levels that here is the open door to this great temple of love.

Call to the mighty archangels to escort your soul there so that you may learn your lessons on the path. We do need archangels and their legions to take us to the retreats, because in order to get to the etheric octave we must pass through the astral plane, the frequency of time and space just above the physical. This realm is very dense and dark because it has been muddied by the impure thought and feeling patterns, conscious and unconscious, of mankind. Without the angels' guidance and protection our soul could become entangled there, and so we call to the legions of Archangel Michael to escort us.

In their retreat, Chamuel and Charity teach lessons in mercy, compassion, and loving care. They also teach you to replace a sense of injustice in relationships with supreme trust—trust that in reality there is no injustice anywhere in the universe, trust in the ultimate resolution of divine love. This can happen only when you, in childlike faith, let go of any sense of injustice and let God and his emissaries mete out divine justice.

Chamuel and Charity will teach you how to intensify the flame of love in your heart and to prepare for the descent of the Holy Spirit into your temple. They promise to heal the many layers of the human aura of anyone who offers devotion and service to them. They say:

Each time you offer to God decrees to the violet flame and songs of praise and prayers of heartfelt sincerity, the angels may, in turn, take from your aura and your body some of the burdens that you carry.

If you invite us, we will come home with you. We will help you with difficult situations you may be dealing with among the members of your family. We will help you in problem situations with your neighbors, your relatives, and in the workplace. We will address whatever is most burdensome to your heart. We will even help you find a job— or a parking place! We will do anything you ask, as long as it is lawful for us to do in the sight of God.

Notice that they prefaced their promise with a condition: "If you invite us..." Angels are polite and reverent. Chamuel says:

We respect God's law of freedom that guarantees you free will in all matters. Thus, when you call not, when you invoke not, the angels enter not—even in time of calamity or cataclysm or personal crisis.

God has set his law in motion. And you who abide in this which has been called the footstool kingdom must understand that earth is the footstool of God and of heaven. On earth you are in control. But if you will it so, if you are willing to set your human will aside, then God in you can be in control! But then you must pray as the Saviour did in purest love, "Not my will, but thine be done." And when you do, beloved, the will of God takes command of your life, and angels unseen implement that will step by step as you cooperate with it day by day.

THE PRAYER *of the* HEART

As Chamuel says, we need to call upon the angels to enter our lives. And yet, many people who did not consciously pray to God or his angels have experienced angelic intercession. How does this occur?

At these times, at some level of our being, we are or have

been engaged in interior prayer. Perhaps we've had an ongoing relationship with God and his angels in this and previous lifetimes, even though we are outwardly unaware of it. Or from the level of the subconscious mind our soul has cried out to God, imploring his assistance.

There is also the prayer of the heart that may not even be formulated in words but reaches the throne of grace and receives an immediate response from the heart of God. Even the prayer of an all-consuming desire to liberate loved ones from pain and suffering is answered by God's angelic ministrants.

Rest assured that God always answers the prayer of the heart by way of sending his ministering angels to you. In other words, angels will answer a prayer from *any* level of your being—conscious or unconscious—where you are reaching out to God for help. Because he knows you need this very personal support to get through life, God created the angels to be his extensions in this imperfect world in which we live.

GUARD *the* HEART

Archangel Chamuel and Charity invite you to pray daily to them to protect your physical heart, your heart chakra, and your divine spark. The heart's sensitivity to good and bad vibrations is great, they say, and both thoughts and feelings register on it. They remind you to be wary of evil spirits who would snuff out the spark of divinity that burns on the altar of your heart or who would attempt to make you vulnerable to heart disease, heart ailments and heart attacks.

The ascended masters and archangels teach us about the preciousness of the heart, the guarding of the heart, the stilling of the heart, and the heart as a center and an opening to God. This is important as we become more and more sensitive to the jagged vibrations of the world and the energies of war and hatred. These jagged energies reverberate on the body, soul, chakras, heart. And so we realize how necessary it is to understand the path of the heart. The guarding of the heart is the *key* to the attainment of higher levels of initiation.

If you give praise to God and his angels in prayer and song, the angels will honor you and be with you even as they were with Jesus, Moses, Buddha and so many who have gone before us. Archangel Chamuel and Charity are the facilitators of this veritable rapprochement of your soul with God through the medium of divine love. They teach the way of wholeness— because only through the restoration of wholeness can you come to grips with your psychology.

RESOLVING YOUR PSYCHOLOGY

Your soul is the part of you that went out from the presence of God when you exercised your free will. Thus, you are the only one who can save your soul. How do you bring healing and resolution to your soul?

The term *inner child* is another name for the soul. Ultimately, to become whole, your inner child must become one with your inner, loving adult. And for that to happen, your inner adult must be loving.

What causes the inner adult to be unloving? Your inner adult is formed and patterned after the model of your parents. If you had perfect parents, your inner adult would be perfect too. But if your parents were not perfect, then you'll need to work at remolding your inner adult, as well as your inner child, according to the pattern of your Higher Self—your Holy Christ Self. When your inner adult is made whole (by loving your inner child and everyone you meet), then you can merge with your Holy Christ Self.

How do you heal your inner child? You do it through the sacred heart of your Holy Christ Self. You love your inner child and deliver that child of the painful memories that have marred the soul from conception. I recommend several books on the inner child for this important step in your soul growth.[7]

Part of your inner adult and part of your inner child—the parts that have become whole through being loved, through finding the way—have already become one with your Christ Self. It is the injured, bruised part of each that cannot unite with the Christ Self until healed.

As you come to resolution with your parents and the parent within, you see parts of yourself being healed and made whole. The little percentages that are healed can now become one with your Christ Self. In this way, step by step, you pursue the healing of your inner child and inner adult, and the bonding to your Holy Christ Self takes place.

This process of resolution can never be complete unless you are willing to balance the negative karma you have made with those who are closest to you. This means forgiving and forgetting, praying for others, quelling impatience, overcoming insensitivity to others' needs and the sense of injustice, for ultimately there is no injustice anywhere.

We have all made mistakes in the past that require us to serve to set life free—and that means anyone who may come into our life. Admitting our responsibility to right all past wrongs is the first step toward wholeness on the path of divine love. Get into the mode of helping others, going the extra mile, and forgiving seventy times seven.

THE REUNION *of* TWIN FLAMES

Twin flames are divine complements. God created you with another half. From a white-fire body of light, a sphere of wholeness, God created two of you—twins, two halves of the Divine Whole.

While you lived in the levels of perfection, you were always one. When you left the presence of God, somewhere along the way you started making karma with other people. You started getting into other relationships, started quarreling with your twin flame, and you became separated for long centuries. You grew farther and farther apart. Sometimes you may not encounter your twin flame for many lifetimes. You may feel alone without your "other half," and that sense of aloneness can be all-consuming.

Wholeness is a state of being one with God and in harmony with the various compartments of your own self. By engaging in the process of working on yourself daily, you free up your creative energies so that you can attract your twin flame. Unless you establish a direction of wholeness in your life and make inner and outer wholeness a daily priority, you run the risk of your twin flame not recognizing you, or of you not recognizing your twin flame. Wholeness means striving to be who you were in the beginning with your twin flame so you can be together in the reality, not the illusion, of your True Self today.

Archangel Chamuel and Charity are pledged to reunite you with your twin flame if you obey the law of divine love and are willing to balance your karma, even through great sacrifice and hard work. They teach that the way to unite with your twin flame is to first unite with your own God Presence. "In that 'Polestar of Being', in that magnet of sacred fire, you shall become a blazing sun to draw unto yourself" your twin flame. They say that the way to union with your twin flame is to get busy and do the job that you know very well God has assigned you to do. Even if you don't want to, do it with a joyous heart, because it happens to be your karma. Be joyous that you have the opportunity to balance karma every day.

Chamuel and Charity teach:

"That ye love one another as I have loved you" is the word of your Holy Christ Self spoken to you and to your twin flame. For, painful as it might be, you are separated from your twin flame for only one reason: You have not loved one another as Christ has loved you individually, and therefore the karma of non-loving has produced the separation. Let perfect love cast out your fear of being alone, separated from God and your twin flame. Invoke the violet flame with the promise: "O God, never again may I injure my twin flame or any part of life." If you "love one another" as Christ has loved you forever, so it will be counted unto you as the expression of love for your twin flame.

In other words, whoever you are with, in whatever relationship—family, friends, relatives, neighbors, colleagues, co-workers—when you give to everyone the love that you would give to your twin flame, that love does go to your twin flame and is counted toward the restoration.

So when you see people, remember, Christ dwells in them. They have a guardian angel. Give all the abundant love of your heart, and know that this love is never lost, never wasted—no matter what the reaction—because pure divine love always returns to the heart of God after you have sent it through those you are loving.

BALANCE KARMA

Chamuel and Charity tell us, "Love all life free and, you see, you will balance every injustice that has separated from you the beloved of your heart."[8]

Many do not see why they should have to balance their karma. "Jesus has already paid the price for their sins," or so they have been told, and so they walk away from their responsibility—because it is difficult, painful, and unpleasant to be tied to somebody or some situation they just do not like.

Whatever you do, at work or play, don't quit because somebody looks at you the wrong way or speaks to you in a way you don't like. Wherever a disagreement has come between you and another, don't quit until you have sought understanding, peace and at least a mutual respect. When all that can be said has been said, move on. You cannot make people like you, but you can always be kind.

Stick with it and balance your karma by serving to set life free—most importantly those nearest to you. Give decrees or mantras to the violet flame with all due diligence and dedication, and by and by you will balance that karma and never have to deal with that situation and that person again—unless you make more negative karma with that one. You may even find that things between you have so improved, because you have balanced the karma and worked on your psychology, that you can now see the worth of continuing the relationship.

Thus, it is important to accept your karma-balancing

assignments from God. It's also important not to hold on to a false sense of responsibility and stay too long in a situation when you have cleared your karma and transcended the association. Applying all these guidelines can help you balance the karma that separates you from your twin flame.

Perhaps you are sitting next to your twin flame right now. Your karma, whether it is with your twin flame or anybody else, could very well snatch away the relationship you have been waiting for all your life and even for lifetimes. Your karma could also deprive you of a greater intimacy with your chief guardian angel. Yes, karma can rob you of deep and satisfying relationships at all levels.

Until you have balanced 100 percent of your karma, any remaining karma you have is a possible point of separation and division between you and your God, and you and your twin flame. Even though many twin flames are separated in the physical dimension, their souls may be working together in the heaven-world, in the archangels' retreats and in the universities of the Spirit.

PREPARING *for* OUR TESTS

Someone I had not talked to since high school said to me recently, "We're all being tested, aren't we." And I said, "We surely are all being tested."

As the tests advance in this schoolroom of life, we sometimes think it is impossible to know right from wrong. In the moment, when all we have to go by is our relative vision, wrong may seem right, and right may seem wrong.

But we can prepare for those tests and those initiations, which are always the testings of divine love. We can prepare through daily prayer, a habitual going to the heart of God and communing with him, keeping in touch with God. We should also keep in touch with our guardian angel and freely talk with the archangels.

If you have strayed, you can confess this in your heart. Then give your prayers and assign yourself a penance. Tell God and your guardian angel, "I really want to make this right. Let me perform a service or give special prayers or go out and help people in my community, because I don't want this to be a blot on my record." If you keep striving to do the best you know how, you will learn from your mistakes —and not repeat them. You can say, "Okay, I fell in that mud hole, but I am not going to fall in it again. I see that trap and I am not going to fall for it another time."

Life is a schoolroom. God expects that you will make mistakes. But he expects you to not make them too many times. He expects you to get out of the rut and move on, to exercise your inner willpower. And more than that, God expects you to pray to him to strengthen you in the moment when you could fall into that rut again.

Be mindful of your words and actions and even your feelings toward others. When the angels see you self-correcting and trying to do the best you can for everyone, they will give you such support and help. And so, what could have been pain and sorrow becomes a joyous challenging day by day of anything that might assail your path.

As you come to tests or temptations, call upon the legions of divine love. They may come in the softness of the Mother to comfort life, robed in layers of gossamer light as they caress and strengthen those who are weary in their fight for soul freedom. Depending on their assignment, these legions who lovingly administer God's justice may also appear in ceremonial dress or in full battle regalia.

THE RUBY RAY JUDGMENT

It was Archangel Chamuel and Charity who delivered God's judgment at the Tower of Babel. This episode from earth's ancient past is described in Genesis, and I have seen it in the akashic record.* It is truly awe-inspiring to see the record of this mighty archangel standing over the Tower of Babel built by Nimrod to the glory of Nimrod. The ruby ray of the LORD's judgment came down through Chamuel, and in an instant the people were speaking in different tongues.

The ruby ray is an intensification of the pink flame. It is an intense action, like a laser beam. After this judgment descended, all was in chaos. Fear turned to anger—anger against the LORD and his angel. God, acting through his mighty archangel of the third ray, had confounded their speech. They could no longer communicate with each other, and so they could no longer conspire to do evil against God and his people.

Nimrod was a rebel angel whose ambition was to control the world. Rebel angels in high places are a fact of life on planet Earth. They have been here for thousands of years—ever since they lost the war in heaven to Archangel Michael and his legions, who banished them to the earth. Their ambitions have not changed, and they move among us in the same kind of bodies that we have.

---

*Akasha *is primary substance, or etheric energy, that can absorb, or record, all the impressions of life. All that transpires on earth is recorded in a dimension known as akasha.*

Do the archangels and their hosts still wage war with fall-en angels on behalf of the children of light? To answer this question, we look at Jewish mysticism and the system of the Kabbalah.

The ten *sefirot* (plural) that make up the Tree of Life are extensions of the unmanifest God into the manifest world. Each *sefirah* (singular) embodies a quality of God, and togeth-er they display the degrees of divine manifestation.

According to one system of the Kabbalah, Archangel Chamuel embodies Gevurah, "Divine Justice." Thus, Chamuel is perceived as meting out the severity of the judgments of God. But we must remember this comforting scripture: "Whom the Lord loveth he chasteneth, and scourges every son whom he receiveth."[9] When in divine love the Lord metes out his chastenings, we know that Chamuel is bringing us back to Reality, to our Real Self, stripped of all of our sense of human injustice.

THE FALSE HIERARCHY

The fallen angels have attempted to create a false hierarchy that opposes every angel and archangel who is a servant of the light. And so the war does continue. But the impostors of the ray of divine love are no match for the powerful and imposing forces of Chamuel and Charity and the covering cherubim. One glimpse of these fiery pink-, rose- and ruby-colored le-gions as they step out of the Sun and into the lower kingdom, where the warfare of light and darkness continues, and you *know* you are in capable hands.

The archangels and their hosts are still waging war against the rebel angels in the earth and on the lower astral planes—

and the legions of light are winning! You can join them as you champion the cause of children, the poor, the homeless and all who suffer under the yoke of personal and planetary karma.

I once witnessed the protection of a divine angel and the opposition of a very dark angel. I was studying in Boston at the time and took a trip to Cape Cod. I felt an angel of the LORD protecting me and I was in awe in the presence of that good angel. At the same time I felt the force of a fallen angel who was attempting to wrest me from my allegiance to the good angel, and I observed how determined that dark angel was to tear me from the right and true path.

If you have felt the power and presence of an angel defending you and felt the adversary tempting you, then you understand that the reason we sometimes get into trouble is that we go the way of the bad angel, the rebel angel. We consciously reject the angel of light, and therefore that angel withdraws and leaves us to make our karma as we will. The reason we do not all escape the calamities of life or the wrong turns in the road is because the angels respect our free will.

So when you are making a decision that has major consequences or when you come to key turning points in your life, commune with God. Listen to the inner voice and be so close to the altar of God that you have the discernment of spirits from the Holy Spirit. With that discernment, you will truly know right from wrong.

CHALLENGE *the* FORCES *of* ANTI-LOVE

The force of anti-love is anything that opposes the manifestation of God within you—any little irritation, any anger, any argument, any cross words, any passivity that prevents you from getting a job done. It is every force that is anti the light within you, every force that violates the integrity, the honor and the freedom of your soul. It is everything from mild dislike and criticism and condemnation to abject hatred.

Chamuel says these forces of anti-love are subtle, that they are within both the subconscious and the world at large. They have inserted themselves into your psyche through authority figures, for example, who cause you to feel self-dislike, self-condemnation, and an absence of self-worth. All of those negatives come under the heading of the forces of anti-love.

Archangel Chamuel teaches you how to challenge the forces of anti-love. He says: "Purging your house of the force of anti-love is a means of preparing your soul for wholeness and for empowerment by the archangels."[10] Until you rid yourself of these forces of anti-love, the archangels cannot give you the power to achieve and accomplish all the good that you would sponsor. Why? Because so long as you allow anti-love to be part of your household or psyche, then unexpectedly, at any random moment, you could unleash that force of anti-love and abuse the power that God could give you through the archangels.

This is how all of humanity have lost the empowerment of God. This is why our lives have been shortened to threescore and ten. They are being extended somewhat these days, but the Bible describes how people used to live hundreds of years. Some people do not believe that, but I do. In those times, people did not misuse God's power and so they had his power to extend their lives to 110, 180, 200 years and more.[11]

If you are seeking the power of God for a good cause, to make something happen in your town, for example, you need that power and energy. You need that abundance of supply. Therefore you have to tackle the forces that would divide you and cause you to lose God's energy. God is very conservative with his energy. He places it as an investment in people who do not allow themselves to become discordant or angry or even unkind toward anyone.

KEEP *the* VIGIL *with the* ARCHANGELS

Archangel Chamuel is emphatic: He says the seven archangels and their hosts have the solutions to even the most serious problems of our cities and nation, such as organized crime, drugs, illiteracy, gangs, the national debt, AIDS. They have solutions to the problematic elements of your psychology and can show you how to heal them. He promises that if you keep the vigil with the archangels, the solutions to all your problems will be found. Chamuel says:

I, Chamuel, with Charity and all hosts of God, summon you! It does not take twenty-four hours a day. It takes a commitment, even of a small amount of time....

We serve those who are most open to being served because they have opened their hearts to God and are of a devotional nature. Yet we assist all, for the hour of opportunity is at hand, and this opportunity must be seized by every one of you.

Why not commit a minimum of fifteen minutes a day without fail to giving one of your favorite invocations ... just to maintain your tie to us so that waking or sleeping we may pass the light through your chakras and bring resolution day by day.[12]

CHAMUEL *and* CHARITY

RAY AND COLOR	*Third ray, pink to rose to ruby*
QUALITIES	*Love, creativity and beauty*
CHAKRA	*Heart – 12 petals*
PROMINENT ON	*Monday*
SPIRITUAL RETREAT	*Over Saint Louis, Missouri, USA*

ASK THEM FOR:

SPIRITUAL GIFTS	*Love, compassion, mercy, forgiveness of self and others; creativity; true understanding of selflessness, self-love, self-acceptance, self-esteem; preparation to receive the Holy Spirit*
PERSONAL ASSISTANCE WITH	*Getting along with others; reunion with your twin flame; starting new relationships and healing existing ones; knowing when and how to end an unhealthy relationship; using loving language; finding a job*
HELP WITH WORLD ISSUES	*Healing relations between races, creeds, nations, ethnic groups*

HEART CHAKRA MEDITATION

Archangel Chamuel teaches that devotion to the Father-Mother God affords protection to your heart and heart chakra. You can use the following mantra to expand and strengthen them. The four lines contain the metaphor and the deep understanding of your soul that your heart is a rose that is unfolding. The fragrance of your heart goes out to God as devotion, and as you pour it forth you can move with that devotion because you are a part of it.

As you give this mantra, place your hands over your heart and visualize your twelve-petaled heart chakra unfolding like a rose. The fragrance of your heart is your devotion to God and your love for all people. Pour forth devotion to God and then visualize yourself one with the whole cosmic ocean of God's consciousness.

> As a rose unfolding fair
> Wafts her fragrance on the air,
> I pour forth to God devotion,
> One now with the Cosmic Ocean.

You can give this prayer as a mantra many times a day as a means of sustaining your tie to God. This is a very profound little mantra. It is one of those mantras of divine love that guards you against the sharp word, something unkind or thoughtless that hurts someone. When you have a momentum

of the mantras of love in your heart, then you are in control
and so you do not let out things that cause burdens to people.
The love mantras are so important.

As you meditate on the God of love while repeating these
four lines, you can actually go into a spiritual ecstasy that
comes from releasing the love in your heart.

BE GONE, FORCES OF ANTI-LOVE!

Chamuel and Charity have given us a mantra that can be used
for the turning back of forces of anti-love in the earth. Chamuel says, "Be prepared to deal with the forces of anti-love that
will not leave you voluntarily. Therefore you must make the
fiat with me: Be gone, forces of anti-love!"[13]

When you give this fiat, Chamuel directs the light through
your chakras and sends it to every nation for the binding of
the forces of anti-love in their governments, their economies,
and all aspects of society. See in your mind's eye the familiar
national landmarks as a point of reference, and add the legions of Chamuel and Charity to those scenes.

Visualize the action taking place instantaneously by millions of legions of angels under Chamuel's command. Use
your third eye to send a beam of light into every nation where
the forces of anti-love are on the rampage. As you watch the
news, you can take notes and record the scenes with your inner sight. Then turn off the news, offer a simple prayer to
God asking for his intercession in all situations you have seen,
and conclude with this fiat:

Beloved Chamuel,
I call to you to give this fiat with me:
In the name of God, I AM THAT I AM,
In the name Archangel Chamuel:
  Be Gone, Forces of Anti-Love!
  Be Gone, Forces of Anti-Love!
  Be Gone, Forces of Anti-Love!

How Angels Help You
Recapture *the* Spirit *of* Joy

5

5

ARCHANGEL GABRIEL *and* HOPE

*A*rchangel Gabriel is your friend. If there is one thing you should remember about him, it is this. He says: "I am your friend. You know me well. And when you see me coming and you are in your light body in the etheric highways you say, 'Hail, Gabriel, friend of old!' And we greet one another as comrades and we embrace."[1]

On another occasion Gabriel promised, "I am Gabriel, Comforter of Life.... I am here and I shall not leave you, each one, until you shall have fulfilled your reason for being."[2]

Archangel Gabriel and Archeia Hope serve on the white ray, which corresponds to the base-of-the-spine chakra. It represents the purity of God, perfection, discipline, joy, and of course, hope. Archeia Hope displaces despair and endows us with hope.

Gabriel and Hope's retreat is between Sacramento and Mount Shasta, California, in the heaven-world on the etheric plane. Gabriel and Hope also serve at the Temple of the Resurrection over the Holy Land and at the Ascension Temple at Luxor, Egypt.

The name Gabriel means "God is my strength" or "man or hero of God." His symbol is the lily. In the Old Testament, Archangel Gabriel is the messenger sent by God to interpret Daniel's visions and to give him understanding and wisdom. Jewish tradition says Gabriel prepared Moses and Joseph, son of Jacob, for leadership.

In rabbinic writings, Gabriel is the prince of justice. In one system of the Kabbalah, Gabriel embodies Yesod, the ninth *sefirah* on the Tree of Life. Yesod is the foundation and represents the procreative life force of the universe.

Muslims call Gabriel the Spirit of Truth. In Islamic tradition he is described as the Angel of Revelation who repeatedly came to instruct the prophets. Muslims believe that Gabriel was the angel who dictated the Koran to Muhammad.

In Christian tradition Gabriel is the Angel of the Annunciation and of the Incarnation. He sponsors the incarnation of the Christ in each of us. Gabriel announced to Zacharias that John the Baptist would be born to his wife, Elizabeth. Gabriel announced to Mary that she would bear the Christ Child, Jesus, and told Joseph that Mary was with child. At the soul level, Gabriel also tells fathers- and mothers-to-be when it is time to conceive and bring forth children.

Archangel Gabriel is the angel of the annunciation of the ascension. He comes to say to you, "In this life God has ordained that you may make your ascension, that you may reunite with him never more to reincarnate, to re-embody." And he says,

I give that annunciation to every son and daughter of God who is destined to ascend. I give it to them in their final embodiment.

Whether they hear it or not, it is delivered to their soul and it is what impels them to know more and want more because they sense that the reunion with God is also the reunion with the twin flame and with the Eternal Guru who is God.

Archangel Gabriel instructs your soul as to how you can walk the path of the ascension. The rite of the ascension, he says, is not reserved for the few. He will teach you how to walk in the footsteps of Jesus Christ, how to balance your karma, how to serve to set life free. Gabriel teaches that if you follow the spiritual path and invoke the violet flame, you can ascend at the end of this life unless severe karma dictates a final embodiment in which you would be required to balance your remaining karma.

Even the ascension is not an end—it is the beginning of your eternal life as a co-creator with God. When you ascend, you are no longer bound to a single planet or confined to a flesh body. You retain your individuality, yet you have a celestial body. You move through the cosmos with the Elohim in ever-new self-transcending creation. There is simply boundless and unlimited opportunity for the expression of freedom.

THE JOYOUS ARCHANGEL

Gabriel calls himself "the joyous archangel." He says in no uncertain terms that there is a war to be won for the saving of your soul, a war that you yourself must wage, and yet this path can still be one of perpetual joy. Gabriel teaches:

It is mandatory that you roll up your sleeves and recognize that you are responsible for each errant footstep [that you have ever taken

in this and all previous lives].... By directing the violet flame ... into those records of those footsteps and all events that ensued thereby, you may balance your karma....

Unless you retrace your footsteps, another may follow them and step into the pitfalls of your former self and former path. This is an age when the true seekers of God must recognize a cosmic accountability for thoughts and feelings sown in the winds.[3]

Gabriel says the path you walk in reaping your karma is not a sorrowful way. It is not one of drudgery. It's a path of perpetual joy, because day by day, by the Holy Spirit's violet transmuting flame, you cast into the sacred fire the debris of your karma of the centuries.

There is joy in this path as no other joy you have ever known.... There is joy in conquering! There is joy in defeating the enemy that lurks within the garments of yourself. Whether it be the enemy of greed, or the enemy of overindulgence in food, as gluttony, whether it be the enemy of selfishness or spiritual blindness—there is a joy in conquering. There is a joy self-fulfilling in becoming all that you are.[4]

One thing I have observed about joy—we need to prime the pump of the well until we finally get the water of joy. We need to embrace a spirit of joy if we wish to receive and hold the joy of angels. Jesus said to his disciples, "that my joy might remain in you, and that your joy might be full."[5] Jesus was in the hour of preparing for his crucifixion and yet he spoke of joy—the joy in his heart, his Sacred Heart, the fiery heart that God has given to all of us.

Bank the fires of the heart with joy to rid yourself of hardness of heart, criticism, condemnation, judgment, and gossip regarding others. Keep your thoughts high, and when you see people coming toward you, don't evaluate or judge them but see them as their inner True Self, their Christ Presence. See the light around them, their angels with them. Reinforce that and greet them with the same joy that Jesus has.

This takes effort. You cannot just paste on the feelings of joy or rely on a formula or a success course. You are a conscious being with the potential to realize God, and you have the free will to do so. If you choose to be grumpy or a sad sack, nobody can do a thing about it, not even an angel who would dance and do cartwheels in front of you all day. If you have made up your mind and that is your freewill choice, the angels will not interfere.

HOLD *the* LIGHT

Archangel Gabriel says that to maintain the spirit of joy you have to learn how to hold onto the light—because your light is your joy and your joy is your light. He says, "To determine to hold light, to have light, to be light, to know the light, and to be the servant of the light even while becoming the master of that light, *this* is the calling of the hour."[6]

How do you do this? Protect the light you have garnered by not misusing it in wrong thoughts, attitudes and deeds. Protect the light in the base-of-the-spine chakra and in all of your chakras. When you give devotions to your I AM Presence, you magnetize that energy and it ascends from the base chakra to the crown chakra.

Gabriel says that the spirit of joy comes to you when light is flowing in your chakras. When you raise the pure light of the base chakra to the crown and hold that light in your chakras, you can be highly creative in your job, in your home, everywhere you go. You are full of ideas because that light is pulsating. Those who conserve the Mother light are the most creative individuals in every field. They are also the most joyous. Joy in the heart is the fire of creativity.

Ask Gabriel and his angels to help you maintain and recapture the joyful spirit, even as they help you to recapture and keep the light. When you protect that light, you have energy, strength, vitality in your being.

This is why we give prayers and mantras of protection to Archangel Michael. The angels cannot lawfully give us any more light on a daily basis than we will protect. If we let our light go down the drain through some argument or discord or problem we're having, God will not keep pouring his light into our vessel, a vessel that continually leaks out the light.

When you are strong because God's light is in you, you can work the works of God. That light nourishes all of your organs. Without that light in flow, Gabriel says, degeneration, decay, disease, and death set in. He says that the flow of light in your chakras from the base to the crown was designed by God to keep you in a state of sheer ecstasy and joy and in perfect health.

YOU CAN WORK *with the* ARCHANGELS

One theme that Gabriel often speaks of is this: God needs you. "There is a partnership to be had with the archangels of God,... working together shoulder to shoulder for the Victory."[7]

God in the heart of an archangel needs your specific command, your certain word in order to take action on your behalf. If you are in trouble and need urgent help, simply

send out an SOS. You can just say, "Archangel Michael, help
me, help me, help me!"

Archangel Gabriel urges us to engage in perpetual prayer.
He says, "Perpetual prayer is the prayer of the heart that does
always pray even while you go about your business and deal
with all those things that are required of your karma."[8]

ANCHOR *the* LIGHT *of the* ANGELS

Gabriel teaches that when you are not centered in your Christ
consciousness, the angels cannot use you to anchor their light
to save the earth. You might wonder how God can use you to
save the earth. Gabriel explains:

> We survey a planet ... as we look to avert natural disaster, loss of
> life, physical epidemic, weather manipulation,... dangerous nuclear
> fallout and radiation entering into the cells of the body.... We take a
> reading within mere seconds.... By the computer of the mind of God,
> we seek out and we find those who are at a certain level of Christ
> consciousness, and instantaneously we direct the flow of light through
> them to avert cataclysm.
>
> A ray of God, as a scanning ray, is able to pinpoint on the planet
> who is able to receive that light that will save lives.... All those who
> measure at that degree of light in that moment then become instru-
> ments.
>
> When you see great cataclysm,... understand that in those hours
> it was because there were not enough souls vibrating at the level of the
> Christ Self [to avert mankind's returning karma as it precipitates in
> the earth].[9]

When you are in the right state of mind, the angels will fill

you with light so you can hold the spiritual balance for your home and your city by the very light that is in you. When you take a day off from your spiritual responsibilities, that day could be the very one on which God would have liked to fill you with his light on behalf of others.

The angels will make of your body an electrode of light. When you feel that light come upon you, make the call or give decrees. Multiply the light and know that God is not giving you light just for your own private use. He is giving you that light because people around you need it and their chakras and their bodies are not able to hold that light.

When you look at the news and see any kind of terrible calamity befalling people, call forth the light and direct it to those people and into that situation. You may be at a distance, but through the news you can get an exact mental photograph of that situation and direct all of your light and decrees to it and send millions of angels to help those people.

Helping others makes life worth living. The angels are there. You are the beloved sons and daughters of God. And you *can* do something about world problems. Isn't *that* a cause for joy!

GABRIEL IS YOUR FRIEND

Over the years I have developed a very close personal relationship with Archangel Gabriel simply by tugging on his garment all the time. You can do the same. You just have to prime the pump. Do this with any of the archangels and you will see how swiftly they will respond to your calls.

I would like to tell you about a request I once made of Archangel Gabriel. I received a call from a mother whose son of about seven or eight had been shot at close range with a .30-06 rifle by the neighborhood bully. As soon as I received the phone call, I called to Archangel Gabriel. I made a deep, intense heart call to him that I will never forget. I was absolutely determined in my heart that Gabriel would come and that he would save this child's life. Not for one moment did I ever doubt it, because I know Archangel Gabriel and I know he keeps his promises.

I saw Gabriel step out of the Sun in answer to my call and descend to the side of this child. The bullet had entered the child's right side, gone through his liver and spleen, passed within three-eighths of an inch of his heart, shattered his elbow, and lodged in his wrist. Daily I kept the vigil. I visualized this boy absolutely whole, absolutely perfect in every place where this bullet had passed.

Once a day I stopped everything and concentrated on Gabriel and this boy and gave my fervent heart calls to God. Someone had to give Gabriel the authority to act and intercede on earth. This is the law of free will. When you are keeping the vigil for someone who has a serious physical problem, you must tend the flame at least once in each twenty-four hours.

Each and every day for months, I saw Archangel Gabriel minister to this child while he went through operations, hospitalizations and convalescence. The doctors said the only reason he survived was his "will to live." The child came to be known as the miracle child of Kootenai Hospital in Idaho.

Then came the day when I was in California at our church there. I conducted an Easter sunrise service, and when this little child came through the line with his grandmother to receive Holy Communion, I looked at him with such joy in my heart. I could not hold back the tears. All I could say to him was, "Are you whole?" And he said, "Yes, I am whole."

NEVER GIVE UP
This incident reinforced for me the simple but profound message we often hear from Gabriel's divine complement, the archeia Hope. The message is *Never give up*. Hope says:

> *Understand, then, why the flame of hope is my charge and destiny. For to keep alive but a flicker of hope in the hearts of the children of the Sun ... is to preserve the opening for the entrée of the Lord Christ or any angel or cosmic being into the world of that one.*[10]

Hope says that she and Gabriel and their angels work to expand "a purity that is like steel." She says, "Can you imagine compressed light so fiery as to be stronger than the strongest wall, harder than the hardest hardness known? It is the concentration of light that does make the aura impervious to despair."[11]

You must be impervious to despair. Don't allow depression or a sense of hopelessness to creep in to your heart or your mind or your soul. The moment you feel a little bit negative, a little bit down, put on your tube of light* and call to the angels to bind those demons of despair. Call to Archeia Hope to fill you with hope.

Archeia Hope says you must beware of false and misplaced hope, hope that you place in individuals who do not have a tie

*See page 58.

to God and only bring disillusionment. Trust in God, hope in him, and commend all people to him, but do not put your trust and faith in mortals. Your hope is in God—and he will not fail you. Archeia Hope teaches:

It is important to hope in the realm of the possible. For if you continually hope for that which cannot be, for it violates the Law or is not practical or probable,... you will soon be lost in daydreams and fantasies where nothing comes to pass. Thus, beloved, the secret of hoping and rejoicing in hope is to hope for those things which you know can, should, must, shall, and are now presently possible for you.[12]

GABRIEL *and* HOPE

RAY AND COLOR	*Fourth ray, white*
QUALITIES	*Purity, discipline, ascension, perfection, hope, joy*
CHAKRA	*Base of the Spine – 4 petals*
PROMINENT ON	*Friday*
SPIRITUAL RETREAT	*Over the area between Sacramento and Mount Shasta, California, USA*

ASK THEM FOR:

SPIRITUAL GIFTS	*Guidance in creating your spiritual life; revelation of your life plan and purpose; joy and fulfillment; preparation for your ascension, sense of holiness*
PERSONAL ASSISTANCE WITH	*Establishing discipline and order in your life; organizing your emotional, mental and physical environments; new directions in your education and career*
HELP WITH WORLD ISSUES	*Peacekeeping operations; distribution of food, medical assistance and relief for victims of natural and manmade disasters*

COMMUNING with ANGELS of PURITY

ARCHANGEL GABRIEL'S EXERCISE
TO SEAL THE CHAKRAS

Archangel Gabriel teaches an exercise for holding the light of joy and sealing your chakras.

Center your love in your heart. Feel the fire of God intensifying in your heart. See it as white fire becoming pink, the color of the heart chakra, the color of love.

Place your left hand over your heart and your right hand over the left. Visualize yourself drawing out of your heart with your right hand a white disc about the size of a saucer. Gabriel calls this white disc "an electrode of energy."

Still holding your left hand on your heart, place your right hand one to two inches above your crown chakra. With your left hand you are drawing energy from your heart, and with your right hand you are placing this energy over the crown chakra.

Now close your eyes and visualize this white disc over the crown. It is a disc of light charging your crown chakra. You can move your hand in a slight clockwise motion. Visualize the white disc over the crown, intense white fire as brilliant as the sun shining on new-fallen snow. You may feel your crown chakra tingling from the light.

When you feel that you have made that contact and it is intense enough (or when you feel ready to move on), leave your left hand over your heart and move your right hand to about an inch in front of your third eye and repeat the motion and visualization as for the crown chakra. Be in a receptive mode to this light. Receive the light. Open your heart to the light, open your crown and your third eye.

If you are able to feel the tingling in your third eye, then when it has reached its peak (or when you feel ready), take your right hand and put it in front of your throat chakra and do the same thing.

When you have accomplished this, move your hand to about an inch over your heart. Take a few deep breaths. Feel yourself charging your heart—your physical heart and your heart chakra. This is a guarding action, an invigorating action, a sealing action.

When you have completed the heart, go to the point of the navel, your solar-plexus chakra. Feel the light going in and establishing absolute peace as you rotate your right hand over the navel area. Let go all that is not at peace in your world. Let the fire consume all disagreements, friction, unresolved problems. Accept the gift of Cosmic Christ peace at the level of your solar-plexus chakra.

Now go to the seat-of-the-soul chakra, which is midway between the navel and the base of the spine. Visualize this dazzling white saucer over the seat-of-the-soul chakra. Reassure your soul: "O soul of mine, be at peace. O soul of mine, be at peace. O soul of mine, be at peace."

Now go to the base of the spine and seal the four petals, the white fire, the Mother light of the base-of-the-spine chakra.

Now, keeping your left hand over the heart, take your right hand and raise it slowly up the line of your chakras, pausing briefly at each chakra. You can do this several times, slowly, beginning at your base chakra. Seal and raise the light. Consciously will it to rise. After you've raised your right hand to your crown chakra, place it over your heart again to complete the ritual. Then, if you are so inclined, chant the Om.

Try this exercise upon awakening. Before you even get out of bed in the morning, you can do this entire exercise. You can do it whenever your chakras need a recharge.

We all know the feeling of being in a state of happiness and then along comes someone who is in a funk or under a cloud. They have nothing positive to say about anything or anyone. All of a sudden your smile turns down and you feel kind of glum. Archangel Gabriel says that is when you need to invoke your tube of light, call for the violet flame, and seal your chakras with this exercise. He says that this is something you can do several times a day, especially when you feel drained after being in a crowd.

THE LIGHT OF THE ASCENSION

Archangel Gabriel teaches us that the ascension is the goal of life. When we walk this path, we are, in fact, ascending by increments every day by our good words and good works, our mantras, the desiring of our heart, and the positive light we send forth. When you give a decree such as the one below, a portion of yourself returns to God; it's not a sudden process. You are participating in the grand ritual of being born again fully in the Spirit as an individualization of the God flame.

This is an affirmation of what is to be—which means it always has been and is now—and yet in our experience as finite beings we must go through the process, the cycle, the ritual. That is why we have a matter universe. Remember, "I AM ascension light" means "God in me is ascension light."

Ascension

I AM ascension light,
Victory flowing free,
All of good won at last
For all eternity.

I AM light, all weights are gone.
Into the air I raise;
To all I pour with full God-power
My wondrous song of praise.

All hail! I AM the living Christ,
The ever-loving One,
Ascended now with full God-power,
I AM a blazing sun!

How Angels Help You
Heal Yourself *and* Others

6

ARCHANGEL RAPHAEL *and* MOTHER MARY

*T*he archangel of the fifth ray is Raphael and the archeia is Mary, the mother of Jesus. How did the Blessed Mother become the archeia of the fifth ray?

In fact, Mary has been an archeia and the divine complement of Raphael from the moment that God created archangels. We cannot even calculate in cycles of the earth or the sun their ageless presence in the universe.

Many ages ago, Alpha and Omega, the Father-Mother God, gave Mary the commission, if she would accept it, to take embodiment in human form to be the mother of Jesus. The assignment was given to Raphael to remain in heaven and to hold the balance for Mary, supporting her from the octaves of light while she was on earth.

And so Mary was born in the earth and she did give birth to Jesus. Some say she embodied a number of times, in ancient times in the golden ages of Atlantis, giving birth to the same soul that we know as Jesus. It is my understanding that Jesus had lived many lifetimes, even as we have lived many lifetimes. At the conclusion of her life as Jesus' mother, her divine plan fulfilled, Mary made her ascension.

Archangel Raphael and Mary have their retreat in the etheric realm over Fátima, Portugal. Mary also serves at the Resurrection Temple, an etheric retreat over the Holy Land.

The fifth ray, or green ray, is the ray of healing, music, truth, the precipitation of the abundant life, mathematics, science, and the Word of God. This ray corresponds to the vision of God and the third-eye chakra, right at the point of the brow. Through this ray we are able to precipitate in form all that we would bless the earth with by our efforts, our prayers and our diligent service. We feel the expression of the green ray most strongly on Wednesday, the day on which many churches hold healing services.

RAPHAEL *in the* WORLD'S RELIGIONS

The name Raphael means "God has healed," or "the Medicine of God." Some traditions call Raphael the angel of science and knowledge and the guardian of the tree of life in the Garden of Eden. Jewish texts say that Raphael banished the demons in the earth after the flood of Noah and revealed to Noah the curative power of plants. Many commentators identify Raphael as the angel who troubled the waters at the pool of Bethesda, where Jesus healed the impotent man.

The Book of Enoch describes Raphael as the angel who presides over the diseases and wounds of men. In this text, Raphael is commissioned to punish one of the rebel angels and heal the earth of their defilements. He is also described as a guide in the underworld.

A Jewish tradition names Raphael as one of three archangels who appeared to Abraham in the plains of Mamre. It is also believed that Raphael endowed Sarah with the strength to conceive when she was past childbearing age. In one system of the Kabbalah, Raphael is said to embody the eighth *sefirot*, Hod, which is "Majesty" and "Splendor." The poet Longfellow, in *The Golden Legend*, describes Archangel Raphael as the Angel of the Sun.

Evidence of veneration of Archangel Raphael is infrequent before the sixteenth century. By the seventeenth century, the Church often dedicated masses to him. Raphael's feast day is September 29. He is known as chief of the guardian angels and the patron of travelers.

In works of art, Raphael is often portrayed wearing sandals and holding a pilgrim's staff, an image derived from his role in the Book of Tobit. This scripture is included in the Catholic Bible, but in the Protestant tradition it is found in the Apocrypha. Scholars believe that Tobit was written in the second or third century B.C. During this period in Judaism, reverence for angels was increasing. In the Book of Tobit, God sends Raphael to alleviate the suffering of a pious Israelite family living in exile.

WALKING *with* RAPHAEL

The Book of Tobit tells the story of the young man Tobias and his father, Tobit, who is blind. Tobit sends Tobias to recover a deposit of money in a far city. Raphael, disguised as a knowledgeable traveler, offers to be his guide. Accompanied by Tobias's dog, they set off together on their journey. On their first night's stop, when Tobias goes to the river to wash, he is attacked by a fish. Raphael tells him to catch the fish and remove its gall, heart and liver. Tobias carries all this with him for the rest of the 325-mile journey to the capital of Media, east of Assyria.

Along the way, Raphael tells him that his next of kin, Sarah, whom he is to meet in the city, is to be his bride. Tobias protests, because Sarah's seven previous husbands have all perished on their wedding night at the hand of the demon Asmodeus. So Raphael gives Tobias a formula that he promises will exorcise Sarah's demon. "When you enter the bridal chamber," Raphael says, "take some of the fish's liver and heart, and put them on the embers of the incense. The reek will rise, the demon will smell it and flee, and there is no danger that he will ever be found near the girl again."

The courageous Tobias marries Sarah, enters the wedding chamber armed with the heart and liver of the fish, and follows Raphael's instructions. Meanwhile, Sarah's father digs a grave for his son-in-law. As the angel prophesied, the reek of the fish sends the demon fleeing through the air to Egypt. Raphael chases the demon and shackles him.

Sarah's parents, elated that he has survived, give the new couple half of all their belongings and treat them to an extended wedding feast. While he is celebrating, Tobias sends Raphael to retrieve Tobit's money. After fourteen days of feasting, the newlyweds and Raphael set off for Tobit's house. On the way, Raphael suggests that he and Tobias travel ahead to relieve Tobias's parents' concern for him.

Promising Tobias that his father will be able to see again, Raphael instructs him: "You must put the fish's gall to your father's eyes. The medicine will smart and will draw a filmy white skin off his eyes. And your father will no longer be blind but will be able to see the light."

As soon as he arrives home, Tobias applies the fishy paste to his father's eyes. He peels off the filmy skin and his father exclaims, "I see you, my son—the light of my eyes!"

In gratitude, Tobias offers half of his new possessions to Raphael. Raphael refuses, then announces to Tobias and his father: "I was sent to test your faith, and at the same time God sent me to heal you and your daughter-in-law Sarah. I am Raphael, one of the seven angels who stand ever ready to enter the presence of the glory of the Lord. Bless God forevermore.

"When I was with you, I was not acting on my own will, but by the will of God. Bless him each and every day. Sing his praises. I am ascending to him who sent me. Write down all these things that have happened to you."[1]

A fifteenth-century painting by Francesco Botticini shows Tobias walking and talking on the road with the angels as nonchalantly as anyone walking down the street today. Tobias is holding the hand of Raphael, not in the least bit intimidated that he's walking with an angel (see previous page). Gabriel is to Tobias' left and Archangel Michael is on his far right. They are all happily going along the road, having a good time. This is exactly the way God intended things to be—that you could feel that you can put your hand in the hand of an angel and walk down the street and tell him all your troubles and pour out your heart to him.

RAPHAEL *the* HEALER

Archangel Raphael and Mary work with healers in every field. They inspire new cures and alternative healing methods upon scientists, those trained in the healing arts, those in the medical profession. Many avenues of healing are valid. If you learn something about them, you can choose the best type of practitioner and care for specific conditions. Don't hesitate to get multiple opinions.

Whatever avenues of healing you explore, don't discount traditional medical care. When you have a serious condition in your body, consider all of your options. God has released wondrous cures through medical science. These have been dispensations of grace that have prolonged life and make our everyday life worth living.

I say this because some people think prayer alone is sufficient. I think we should pray steadfastly while using the most advanced technology in the healing arts. Raphael's angels overshadow faculties of medical schools and scientists and innovators in every branch of health. He says his angels use "laser technology" to "penetrate to the very core of a cell ... and expand the violet flame from within," and to "seal that cell in the healing thoughtform."[2]

We can ask the angels to overshadow doctors, chiropractors, healers of all kinds. Call especially to Raphael and Mary and their angels—they are master surgeons. Bringing all things together from heaven and earth, we will obtain the best results.

HEALING BODY, MIND *and* SOUL

Raphael has said, "We come for the healing of the soul, for the healing of the mind, for the healing of the heart, knowing full well that all else will follow as the healing of the body.... The only permanent healing, and the healing which is ours to bestow, is a healing unto spiritual as well as physical wholeness."[3]

Mother Mary teaches us,

Remember to call upon God, ourselves, and many angels to bring healing where it is possible. And if the Law does not allow it in the flesh, then call ... for the healing of the soul and the spirit that it might take flight from the body in the end to enter new planes of glory and edification to prepare for a final round [on earth before] the ascension. It is the healing of the whole man that we are about.[4]

The angels can accomplish only what karma will allow—unless by an act of grace or the prayers of many that karma can be set aside. Raphael tells us that few can believe the science of karma. Many do not understand the key role karma plays in whether a person's disease can be cured. The *x* factor of the equation that determines if an individual will recover or pass from the screen of life is often his karmic circumstance.[5]

Karma always comes at an inopportune time. I have never seen karma descend on anyone when it was convenient. That is a good reason to not make negative karma. Karma comes back in such wide-orbed cycles that you could wait ten thousand years before you would meet the karma you made on Atlantis or in ancient civilizations. By the time it comes rolling back you cannot comprehend why God would do such a thing to you—when actually karma is nothing but the causes you have set in motion that will always return to their point of origin.

Sometimes, Raphael explains, the Law decrees that karma must be balanced now. If you do not prepare yourself through devotional prayer, through a contrite heart or invoking the violet flame, or if you are bereft of joy in your work, you may find yourself without enough of God's light in your reservoir to consume the darkness that suddenly and swiftly may be outcropping in your body.

Sometimes people find themselves in other levels, having passed from the screen of life suddenly because they were unable to hold the light necessary to sustain life in their body. You can prepare for the day of urgent need by building up the light in your body and balancing your karma through serving life.

Raphael says, "This is the true meaning of 'work while you have the light,'[6] which Jesus told to his disciples." While you *can* serve and you *can* balance karma, do it. Use those years to get closer and closer to God. Raphael counsels, "Balance your karma while you have the strength" and "can change your personal karmic equation."[7]

Raphael says that every one of us, naked in our souls, must face our God and our karma. So let our souls learn well. The powers of intercession are available but there is a price to be paid.

Think not that the violet flame may be invoked to transmute today some spot or blemish of consciousness and then, when one is free and healed by the violet flame, that one may again indulge in the same pattern of sinfulness and invoke the violet flame again and again [to transmute repetitive sins].[8]

If you misuse the violet flame and take it lightly, then by and by the Law will decree that you no longer be given violet flame. To stop sinning takes your willpower harnessed to the power of God's will. If your heart is right and you are determined, the violet flame will remove forever the sin itself and the blot of sin that is on your record.

Some practitioners of healing use prayer, hypnosis or mental willing to deny that a disease exists. "Just say it isn't real and it doesn't exist." People may heal the condition through denial. But the ascended masters tell us that denial simply pushes the disease back into the astral body or the etheric double, where the karma is lodged.

When this is done, the person looks well, feels well, and does not experience the disease of his karma, but he has not balanced his karma. Karma results in disease so that a person can bear his burden and not have to carry it into the next life. Raphael explains the dangers of these methods of healing:

An individual may suddenly be healed of migraine headaches through hypnosis or other practices of so-called metaphysics.... This may come about rather easily to the practiced one, adept in the uses of these methods. But ... a heavy karma does accrue to such practitioners when the violet flame is not used to consume the record of the cause and core of that karma.[9]

To remove the symptoms of disease without removing the record of its cause in this or a past life does a great disservice to the soul. And the individual who assents to the easy "cure" will see sometime, somewhere, in this or a future life, the same problem coming to the surface to be dealt with as karma that must be transmuted before the physical symptoms permanently disappear.

Western tradition does not teach that we are all responsible for our exercise of free will, for how we use the light of God that flows to us over the crystal cord that you see on the Chart of Your Divine Self (page 9). What we do with that light and that energy, how we qualify it negatively or positively determines what we will deal with tomorrow, in ten years, and beyond this life.

Every one of us can be healed if we apply the violet flame to our physical, mental and psychological problems. That is because the violet flame is given to us for the transmutation of karma. You can transmute your karma before the day descends when you should have some calamity come upon you because of that karma. Give the violet flame decrees for fifteen minutes or half an hour each day. Serve life, do your job joyfully, help people, have a positive mental attitude, and give that to others. That is a karma-balancing mode. The violet flame accelerates the balancing of karma.

MARY, QUEEN *of* ANGELS

The name Mary means "beloved of God." There are hints of Mary's place in the angelic hierarchy in Christian tradition. In the apocryphal text "The Book of John the Evangelist," Jesus describes Mary as an angel: "When my Father thought to send me into the world, he sent his angel before me, by name Mary, to receive me."[10] In Catholic theology Mary is known as the "Queen of Angels."

Devotion to Mary has been associated with thousands of miraculous healings, especially at Lourdes in France, Medjugorje in Bosnia and Herzegovina, and other sites where she has appeared. Mother Mary tells us:

My service to earth is directly dependent upon the call of the devotees. And that call most frequently heard, as you know so well, is the Hail Mary. There has been so much controversy regarding the office of

the Mother of God, confusing the office with my person and considering that somehow in this salutation, the human is made divine.

Beloved ones, I would tell you exactly why the tradition of the call to me was begun. It is not because of my person, but because of my office. It is the office which I occupy as Archeia of the Fifth Ray. And upon this office, beloved Alpha has placed an authority for the divine intercession.

The call made to me is answered by millions of hosts of the Lord who bear the flame of that office, who attend the office, who come to earth to succor souls in my name. Therefore the appeal to Mary ... is to the Mother Ray and to the archeia of the fifth ray. But most specifically, it is a scientific call to that point of my contact with the divinity of our Father and of Brahman—and of the Word which I, too, have become....

I am not only your Mother but your very personal friend. I ask you to take my hand, to take me to your home, to accept me as your friend, not as a remote deity, an icon,... but simply as the handmaid of the Lord.... I am one with whom you can be comfortable. I will sit at your kitchen table and have a cup of tea with you. I will receive whatever offering is precious to you and take it to my heart and give it back to you with the full consecration of my love. I will help you in your daily tasks....

I am a mother of your heart. I am an organizer, an administrator. I am a priestess, and I also lead armies of heaven. You may know me in one or many of my offices but, above all, remember that I assist you in your own path of personal management, organization of your life—the setting of priorities, the use of the hours and of your strength.[11]

MY PERSONAL CONVERSION *to* MARY

I was brought up by European parents of Lutheran background, strictly Protestant. Very early in my life I had spiritual experiences, including recalls of past lives, and I went from church to church searching for someone who could teach me about God.

I loved the Catholic Church. But by the time I was in college I had been indoctrinated to think that it was not correct to call to the saints. When I saw Mother Mary portrayed in the subway with the title "Queen of the Angels," I wondered in my heart how she could allow people to treat her as an idol.

One day I was walking down Commonwealth Avenue in Boston. I looked into the blue sky and saw in front of me Mary, the mother of Jesus. She was so free, so light, like a beautiful maiden. She looked as if she could be my sister. She was wearing white and she had the most beautiful smile. I was thrilled, because in just one glance at her, all of that programmed prejudice dropped from me. I was so happy to have found the real Mother Mary.

I didn't walk, I *ran* to the nearest Catholic Church. I was so happy that I could kneel before her statue knowing that I was not bowing to an icon but beyond it to a real person, a heavenly being and the mother of my Lord. I knelt before her and asked her forgiveness for my state of consciousness. I pledged to her my life and all that I would do. I wanted to become her friend and her servant. And so this began my long association with Mary.

ROSARIES *for the* NEW AGE
In 1972 Mary dictated a series of rosaries to me—one for each day of the week, morning and evening. They are magnificent prayers, alternating the Hail Mary with readings from scripture and prayers dictated by the ascended masters.

When Mother Mary gave me these rosaries she said, "This is how I want you to say the Hail Mary." The prayer that Catholics say ends with the words, "Pray for us sinners, now and at the hour of our death." Mother Mary said:

You are not sinners; you are sons and daughters of God. You may have sinned but you are not sinners. You need me not at the hour of death; you need me at the hour of your victory over sin, disease and death. That is when you must call to me for my reinforcement and my protection.

This is how she asked that the Hail Mary be given:

Hail Mary

Hail, Mary, full of grace
   the Lord is with thee.
Blessed art thou among women
   and blessed is the fruit
   of thy womb, Jesus.

Holy Mary, Mother of God,
Pray for us, sons and daughters of God
Now and at the hour of our victory
Over sin, disease, and death.

RAPHAEL *and* MARY

RAY AND COLOR	*Fifth ray, green*
QUALITIES	*Truth, healing, wholeness, science, music and the abundant life*
CHAKRA	*Third eye – 92 petals*
PROMINENT ON	*Wednesday*
SPIRITUAL RETREAT	*Over Fátima, Portugal*

ASK THEM FOR:

SPIRITUAL GIFTS	*Wholeness, vision, spiritual sight, inspiration of truth*
PERSONAL ASSISTANCE WITH	*Healing of body, mind, soul and spirit; inspiration for the study and practice of music, mathematics, science, traditional and alternative medicine; meeting of physical needs (food, clothing, shelter, source of income, tools of your trade)*
HELP WITH WORLD ISSUES	*Repairing of rifts between nations, healing of those injured on the battlefield, inspiration for new cures for diseases*

COMMUNING *with* ANGELS *of* HEALING

A THOUGHTFORM FOR HEALING

The healing thoughtform was created by the archangels to focus and intensify God's healing light anywhere in the body. Composed of concentric spheres of white, sapphire-blue, and emerald-green sacred fire, it was formulated to restore the inner blueprint and divine wholeness when visualized surrounding and penetrating the cells and atoms of the body or a specific organ.

The white sphere of the thoughtform provides purifying energy to establish the geometry of the original, perfect form that God designed. The blue sphere is for protection, and it is the action of the will of God. It summons atoms, molecules and cells into conformity with the original blueprint. The green sphere is the healing sphere. Blending with the action of the violet flame, it is the miracle of God's immortal life that restores the flow of Spirit though matter and makes it whole.

To use the healing thoughtform, use your mind's eye to visualize the physical organ or part of the body that needs healing. If you have a good anatomy book handy, you can look at the pictures to get an accurate mental image. Visualize the energy of the thoughtform penetrating the cells, the molecules, the very core of the atoms of the part of the body that you place your attention on.

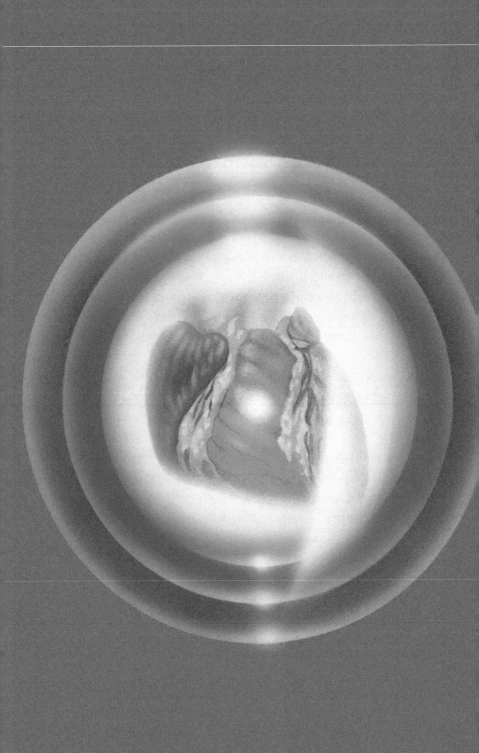

VISUALIZATION AND HEALING

Raphael works with the third eye, and he empowers you to visualize wholeness in yourself and others. When someone is ill or when someone is burdened because of an accident, use the third eye to visualize perfection. Visualize the body healed. Instead of seeing the problem, visualize the results you desire. When you develop the third eye and use it for the power of pure seeing, you will become a healer under the legions of Raphael and Mother Mary.

We call this "holding the immaculate concept," a science that is taught by Mother Mary. Mary teaches us to use our third eye to see the best, the most beautiful, the perfect conception of any part of life. When you look at someone with an eye of love, the eye of God, you see in them the very best. That love sustains your picture of their perfection and it helps them to become it.

If you are with a loved one who has been injured in a major accident, the most important thing that you can do is to keep concentrating on the perfect picture. Keep it steady in your mind's eye. Then repeat the following mantra.

> I AM, I AM beholding All,
> Mine eye is single as I call;
> Raise me now and set me free,
> Thy holy image now to be.

This mantra helps discipline the mind and emotions. It strengthens you to bar the door against your worst fears and to close your mind to all but the most positive affirmations. Still any anxiety, doubt and fear you may have. Keep your eye focused on the image of perfection, not allowing it to move from that image.

Whatever you desire to manifest, see it and visualize it with full concentration during the initial crisis, and later every fifteen minutes, and then every hour. Go to a quiet place and do your work as an alchemist, using the violet flame, using the mind of God that has greater power than anything in this world. Hold the healing thoughtform in your mind to the exclusion of all else and reinforce it with decrees corresponding to each of the elements of the thoughtform—the white light, the blue of protection and the divine blueprint, and the green of healing.

THE EMERALD-GREEN FLAME OF HEALING

This next decree is specifically for healing. The decree includes a preamble that calls upon God, gives direction, and calls for intercession. The body of the decree sustains the action, because as you repeat it you are drawing down the light of God.

When you give a preamble, pour your devotion to God and his angels. As you do this, they will send healing and light back to you on the return current. You have to open the highway to God, and you do this by devotion. So think of yourself as clearing a pathway through the murky substance of the earth plane and all of the density and negative vibrations of your city. Think of yourself carving a tunnel of light directly to the heart of God. Reinforce that opening every day so you feel you have communication with God open all the time.

Flame of Healing

Beloved mighty victorious Presence of God, I AM in me, O thou beloved immortal victorious threefold flame of eternal truth within my heart, Holy Christ Selves of all mankind, beloved Alpha and Omega, beloved Helios and Vesta, Archangel Raphael and the healing angels, beloved Jesus the Christ, Mother Mary and Saint Germain, in the name of the Presence of God which I AM and through the magnetic power of the sacred fire vested in me, I decree:

    1. Healing flame of brightest green,
        I AM God Presence all serene,
        Through me pour thy mercy light,
        Now let truth make all things right.

Refrain: Flame of consecration wonder,
          Let my mind on thee now ponder
          Service to my brother stronger
          And the fullness of thy power.

Flame of consecration healing,
Keep my being full of healing,
Mercy to my brothers sealing
By the grace of God-desire.

2. Flame of healing, fill my form,
   Vibrant life in me reborn;
   God within me, make me whole,
   I AM healing every soul.

In your invocation, you can call forth this healing action
for one person or ten thousand people. Remember that you
can always maximize your call. Use the power of your vision to
visualize every word taking place and manifesting. Accept that
action in full faith for that loved one. Have no shadow of a
doubt, because the healing angels are at work. Then say this
decree with the authority of the Word of God within you. When
you have used this decree for a while and you know the words,
you can say it with your eyes closed and your entire attention
on visualizing what you desire to see physically manifest.

I have received reams and reams of testimonies from
people around the world who have been healed by the calls to
God and the angels' intercession. There is no question that
this science works.

How Angels Help You Create
Personal *and* Planetary Change

7

ARCHANGEL URIEL *and* AURORA

Wherever you may go, even in outer space, you may meet the angels. *Parade Magazine* told this story of an encounter with angels:

> *Six Soviet cosmonauts said they witnessed the most awe-inspiring spectacle ever encountered in space: A band of glowing angels with wings as big as jumbo jets.*
>
> *According to* Weekly World News, *three cosmonauts said they first saw the celestial beings in July 1985 during their 155th day aboard the* Salyut 7 *space station. They said they saw seven giant figures in the form of humans but with wings and mist-like halos and round faces with cherubic smiles, as in the classic depiction of angels. Twelve days later the figures returned and were seen by three other Soviet scientists, including a woman cosmonaut. "They were smiling," she said, "as though they shared in a glorious secret."[1]*

Never underestimate where you might meet an angel. They will make their statement wherever they find a receptive heart, for they love everyone, everywhere.

Uriel and Aurora are the archangel and archeia who serve on the sixth ray of God's peace, brotherhood, ministration and service. The administration of divine justice is also associated with this ray. The color of the ray is purple and gold flecked with ruby. In the archeia Aurora, this color can appear more like the golden-pink glow of the dawn. Uriel and Aurora's work corresponds to the solarplexus chakra, the place of desire and the ultimate place of peace. Their retreat is in the heaven-world approximately over the Tatra Mountains, south of Cracow, Poland.

ANGELS *of* PEACE *and* BROTHERHOOD

The name Uriel means "fire of God," "flame of God" or "God is my light." In Jewish tradition Archangel Uriel is called the "one who brings light to Israel."

Archangel Uriel is not named in the Bible but he is mentioned in other Jewish and Christian texts. In these he is variously identified as a seraph, as one of the cherubim God placed at the east of the Garden of Eden, as an angel of the presence, or as the watcher over the world and over the lowest part of Hades. In the Book of Enoch, Uriel is one of the four chief angels, along with Michael, Gabriel and Raphael. In that text Uriel is Enoch's guide on his journeys through heaven and the underworld. Some traditions say that Uriel warned Noah of the impending flood and that he was sent to teach Noah how to survive the flood.

Uriel is described as the interpreter of prophecies and is often portrayed carrying a book or a papyrus scroll. John Milton describes him in *Paradise Lost* as the "regent of the sun" and "the sharpest-sighted spirit in all of Heaven." In Gnostic

writings Uriel is called Suriel, and he rules over one of the seven planetary spheres. In Islam, Uriel is identified as one of the four angels who guard the throne of Allah.

Uriel is named as one of the angels who lead souls to judgment in the *Sibylline Oracles*, early texts that were used to spread Jewish and Christian doctrine among pagans. These works contain predictions of woes and disasters that will come upon mankind, and they were quoted hundreds of times by the Church Fathers. The second book of the *Sibylline Oracles* says:

> *The imperishable angels of immortal God, Michael, Gabriel, Raphael and Uriel, who know what evils anyone did previously, lead all the souls of men from the murky dark to judgment, to the tribunal of the great immortal God....*
>
> *Then Uriel, the great angel, will break the gigantic bolts, of unyielding and unbreakable steel, of the gates of Hades;... he will throw them wide open and will lead all the mournful forms to judgment, especially those of ancient phantoms, Titans and Giants and such as the Flood destroyed. Also those whom the wave of the sea destroyed in the oceans, and as many as wild beasts and serpents and birds devoured; all these he will call to the tribunal.* [2]

Uriel plays a key role in the apocryphal work *The Fourth Book of Ezra*, considered one of the finest works in Jewish literature. It was so influential in the early Christian Church that it was used in liturgy. It also shaped beliefs in the Middle Ages about the end times. In this book Uriel interprets Ezra's visions and instructs him in the secrets of the universe. He also answers his questions about the judgment of man, the signs of the approaching end of the age, whether the righteous can intercede for the ungodly, and the fate of the wicked.

CHURCH COUNCILS BAN ANGEL WORSHIP

Early leaders of the Christian Church encouraged praying to the angels and approved of devotion to them. Then, in the fourth century, the Synod of Laodicea decided that the veneration of angels detracted from the proper worship of Christ and forbade Christians to worship angels privately outside the walls of the church. It also banned the naming of any angels not specifically mentioned in Catholic scripture. That meant only the archangels Michael, Gabriel and Raphael could be named in prayer—in spite of the fact that Uriel is mentioned in several ancient texts and was known to the Jews and early Christians.

Despite the synod's condemnation, angel worship still flourished. In the eighth, ninth and fifteenth centuries the Church again banned the worship of angels not specifically named in scripture. And as recently as 1950 the pope restricted the adoration of angels, reaffirming that only Michael, Gabriel and Raphael could be named by Catholics. The decrees of these church councils have, in effect, robbed Christians of the knowledge of how to invoke the intercession of these heavenly emissaries just when they need it most.

Papal bans notwithstanding, Archangel Uriel himself encourages you to call upon him by name and to enlist his legions of angels to bring about personal and planetary change. In one dictation Uriel said:

In every world religion angels have been eclipsed and therefore you have been stripped of your intercessors. These are your companions, your brothers, your sisters, your servants.

We are in your midst. We are sent to perform this work. [This is our mission.] We can do the job! We are trained! We are professionals!... Only call to us in the name of God I AM THAT I AM, in the name of his Son Jesus Christ. Then stand fast and behold the salvation of your God![3] Stand fast and see the healing of the nations![4]

A PRAYER *to the* ANGELS CAN SAVE *a* LIFE

Chris Merkel was a young man saved from death when he called out to God to send an angel to rescue him. This story was published in *Guideposts*.

As a youngster Chris believed in angels, because his mother told him they were real. He said he began to doubt their existence when he became a teenager—no one he knew had seen one. But that didn't discourage his mother, who continued to ask God to assign an angel to watch over each of her children.

In January 1991 Chris found reason to rethink his doubts about angels. One day as he got ready for work he heard his mother saying her daily prayers in the kitchen, asking God to send angels to protect Chris at his job. That amused the skeptical Chris.

Chris went to his excavating job. That day he was laying pipe at the bottom of a trench with a coworker, Terry. Suddenly a solid wall of earth came crashing down on them. "Everything was black," Chris says. "Frantically spitting dirt from my mouth, I found my face in an air pocket. The crushing pressure made every breath a struggle. At least I had air, but there was no telling how long it would last as the dirt settled. I was being slowly smothered to death."

As Chris began to lose consciousness, he cried to God to

send them a rescuing angel. Before the rescuers dug him out, he said he felt himself being mysteriously lifted up. He relaxed and passed out. When he came to, he and his coworker were both alive, although the doctor didn't know why they weren't dead. They had been buried for over two hours. "Someone sure must have been looking out for you fellas," he said.

Since then Chris has searched the Bible for every mention about angels. And, like his mother, he now says a daily morning prayer asking God to assign an angel to all his coworkers and every piece of their equipment. "There's no sense in not using what God has given us to use."[5]

I pray you will not wait for a life-and-death crisis to learn the lesson Chris Merkel learned.

ASK ANGELS *for the* ASSISTANCE YOU NEED

Archangel Uriel reminds us that for the archangels to intercede for us, we must submit to the will of God. They will not assist us in doing something that is not God's will. In fact, by not cooperating with that plan they make known to us that perhaps that plan is not God's will.

Uriel says: "We are archangels serving the will of God ... and we come to serve the sons and daughters of God" who are obedient to his will in matters small and great. "We may not, by the law of God, intercede in your life or interfere unless you surrender that human will and say: 'Not my will, but thine be done. O Lord, come into my life and help me!'"[6]

Sometimes we make mistakes and think we do God's will but we err. We can learn from those well-intended but mistaken actions. And by developing the listening grace of the Mother of Jesus, listening to the voice of God inside of us and making

time every day, quiet and undisturbed, just for listening, we become more sensitive to God's will.

Two very important times for listening are the first five or ten minutes after you awaken and as you are falling asleep. At those times you are making the transition between the octaves of the heaven-world and earth, and that's when you may get some of your most important ideas. Those are brief moments, so make additional time to listen to God.

HOW *to* OVERCOME BAD HABITS

Archangel Uriel advises you to zero in on a single condition in your life that you may have been wrestling with for a long time. He says, "Whatever the struggle is—whether it be gluttony or greed or something known only to you and me in the privacy of your own heart":

First, "Be free of all self-condemnation for that condition."

Second, "See yourself in your great Reality, large as life, filled with the Spirit, and look at this problem as an inch high. Have the sense of the power of God in you!"

Third, "Form and draw together in the heart, in the desire body, and in the will a determination that allows the fiat to go forth from your heart in the spoken Word." This is the fiat that Uriel gives you: "O my God, I will have the victory over this beast of my lesser self!"

Fourth, Do not suppress negatives but let them pass into the violet flame. Visualize a river of violet flame moving swiftly in front of you, and then throw your negatives into it and watch them be carried downstream in the violet flame. Just let them pass into the flame right as you invoke it. Uriel says:

Transmutation has a logic all its own. If you would transmute, you must also atone and exchange the lesser desire for the greater. Thus, replace untoward activities and desires with new activities, new joy, new interactions, and friends of light. Take up … sports or hobbies or activities of union, fighting for the freedom of those who need your help right in your own city.[7]

Let this uniting for a cause replace the former self-indulgent activities. You will find that you are so preoccupied in helping others and you are having such a good time channeling your energy into this new and joyous endeavor that you will not regress into old negative patterns when the old emotions surface.

Instead of feeling defeated by a return of old habits, you will be God-victorious because you have focused an iron-will determination in your heart. Good habits are the garments worn by saints. Bad habits are momentums of indulgence that shroud the chakras. Rechannel the stream, reverse the course of your downward momentums, and build a new streambed, directing the course of your life where *you* want to go.

It does require effort—joyous effort—but not martyrdom to transmute your base metals into gold, to atone for misdeeds and mistakes, and to exchange the lesser desire for the greater desire. The archangels are telling us: "We are here to help you. Just call on us and we will prove it to you."

URIEL'S FIVE KEYS *to* CHANGING YOUR LIFE

Archangel Uriel gives you five keys to changing your life, your family, your community and your planet.

1. Call to the seven archangels to infuse your chakras with the light of the Universal Christ.

The seven chakras are used by the seven archangels to anchor light in your four lower bodies—the etheric, mental, desire, and physical bodies. These four sheaths surround the soul, providing vehicles for the soul in her journey through time and space.

The cord of light descending from your I AM Presence is a river of light. So your chakras are being nourished from above, from your I AM Presence, over this crystal cord. They are also being nourished from the base chakra, where there is stored the tightly coiled energy of the light of the Mother. When you raise up this light of the Mother and pull down the light of the Father from your I AM Presence, you have the balance in your chakras of Alpha and Omega, or the plus and minus of the Great Tao.

In the course of our lives, we have correctly used our chakras as well as misused them. There are many ways to misuse that life force, including anger, argumentation and similar negative moods that people exhibit. Those who get into that type of energy can squander a great deal of light in a short time.

People who are in the very bowels of anger and bitterness against life or against God or who are in intense condemnation of others or of people in general are really to be pitied. They are at the mercy of the momentums of their own anger that they have never resolved. Anger can take a person right off the spiritual path.

Your spiritual centers are sacred and you must keep them shielded and in the holiness of God. Call to the violet flame to transmute the improper uses of the light in each of your chakras. Give a prayer like this one to invoke the seven archangels and their light to clear your chakras of these misuses of energy:

Beloved Mighty I AM Presence, beloved seven archangels, infuse now my spiritual centers with the light of the Universal Christ. Purge them first of the forces of Antichrist that may have implanted themselves within me. Purge and purify me now by the power of the Cosmic Christ, by the power of my I AM Presence that I might truly be a chalice for the Lord.

Conserving your sacred fire and life force is so important. Your chakras are sending stations that God uses and that you use to concentrate your light, to conserve energy so that you have it there when you need to direct God's light through your decrees into problem situations in your life and on the planet.

It is up to sons and daughters of God, one with their Christ Presence, to command angels, to give them directions, to pray to them, to call to them for all the assistance we need. We cannot save the world or even save ourselves. But we can call to the angels—they are trained to do that job. Uriel says:

The saints who have prayed daily throughout history are those who have been open hearts to our coming and through them the light has shone. Yet, I tell you, if you are not saints today, you may be saints tomorrow. And the process of sainthood is the infusion of your being and your spiritual centers with the light of the Universal Christ.[8]

2. Apply the violet flame daily and generously.

The violet flame is the gift of the Holy Spirit that comes to us under the sponsorship of the ascended master Saint Germain. The violet flame is a "physical flame" and thus the antidote for physical problems. Visualize yourself or others saturated with violet flame. The more specific you are in your visualization, the more immediate the response and the action. This is especially helpful when you are praying for yourself or others in case of accidents, surgery or serious illnesses.

If you can, get an exact description of the condition. This will tell you where and how to direct the violet flame. Make a specific call to God to focus the violet flame in the areas of need, then hold a strong visualization of the violet flame penetrating those places.[9] And remember, the violet flame is an adjunct to sound scientific measures, not a substitute for them. Consult your doctor and take the remedies that are specific for your problem.

The violet flame can also clear the records of negative karma —including the records of our own and others' misdeeds. For instance, Archangel Uriel says it is important to clear the records of death and war on the battlefields of the planet in order to ensure peace on the earth.

3. Increase the flame of peace in your aura.

Uriel says that if you want to keep the peace in your life and in your home, he will teach you how to use the power of peace to wage war against the forces of anti-peace that lurk both inside and outside of yourself.

Many states of consciousness are anti-peace. Most notable among these are what I call the Martian "A's," all the negative energies associated with the planet Mars: anger and agitation in the feeling world, argumentative or accusative attitudes, feelings of annoyance or aggravation; all forms of physical and psychic aggressive-compulsive behavior; and everything from apathy to a tendency toward total self-annihilation. In sum, the forces of anti-peace include any condition where you lose your equilibrium and in the resulting unbalanced state lose your harmony and allow any of the above to be expressed through you.

On each occasion Uriel advises us: Return to God-harmony as fast as you can. "*Return to God-harmony … in the tone of the voice, in the thoughts of the mind, in the feelings that go forth.*"[10] The state of God-harmony is when you have absolute God-control over the energies that are passing through you. He admonishes you to rise to the plane of your Christ Self and no longer allow the different parts of yourself, as spoiled children, to pull you in four directions. The power of God is to be found in the inner stillness of the heart. Seek it and you shall find it.

4. Invoke the Lord's judgment and the resurrection.

The fourth key Archangel Uriel gives to bring about personal and planetary change has two steps: *invoke the power of the Lord's judgment*; and *invoke the power of the Lord's resurrection*.

Archangel Uriel has delivered many dictations through me and through Mark Prophet for the judgment of conditions of evil in our society. Call to him to bind the forces of injustice. He says:

I am that one who listens day and night…. I wait for someone to make the call for the binding of the horrendous injustices upon this planet!... I tell you, there is a higher court where matters are adjudicated swiftly and finally and the karma does descend. Therefore be healed of any sense of injustice about anything in you, outside of you or in the land or in the world. Simply invoke the Lords of Karma and remember, Uriel is waiting to be called into action![11]

Uriel explains that those who receive God's judgment through the archangels are given a window of opportunity to turn around and worship the living God. The judgment of an individual, then, is not the end of the individual. It is the judgment of certain actions whereby a person's karma may come upon him to teach him lessons.

You can call for the judgment of negative personal and planetary conditions around you. You can also apply the action of judgment to your own not-self, the self that is the antithesis of your Higher Self. When you ask God to judge you, his sacred fire descends into your temple, not to harm you but to separate the bad elements from the good. By this means you can see error or bad habits for what they are: no part of your Real Self.

When you call to Uriel for divine justice and judgment, you may not witness an immediate answer to your call. When that justice is released, change begins deep within the psyche of man and society. God begins to resolve the intricacies of an injustice deep from within, at unconscious levels. You may only see resolution when it begins to manifest at the concrete levels of the conscious mind and body. But be assured, the process has begun and it will be fulfilled with or without your knowledge.

When you turn over every sense of injustice to God, you experience a wonderful freedom. But this also requires forgiveness on your part. Sometimes it is difficult to forgive evildoers who do terribly bad things. The key that God has given me is to forgive and pray for mercy for the soul and pray for the binding of the elements of the person that are not under the control of the Christ and therefore have the capacity to work evil.

This is the dichotomy of forgiveness: Some deeds we feel we cannot forgive—these things burn profoundly and deeply. But we can pray for forgiveness for the soul who was the instrument of them, even while we call for the absolute judgment of the aspects of the self that are the antithesis of the Real Self. So you can forgive everyone, turn over all injustices to God, and see how free you will feel.

As you call to Archangel Uriel for the judgment of forces of evil on the planet or of your own not-self, also call for the flame of resurrection. Visualize the resurrection flame—a most beautiful flame with a mother-of-pearl iridescence—bringing renewal, rebirth, rejuvenation, restoration. See it renewing and accelerating every atom, cell and electron of your being.

Archangel Uriel said:

> Understand that this power of the flame of the resurrection, of the angel of the resurrection, and of my heart is for that twofold mission— for the binding, then, of the not-self wherever it does appear, within or without, and for the transmutation [of the karma] of the cities and [the misqualified energy of the people] that that purified place may never, never, never be requalified by the human.[12]

Archangel Uriel will teach you how to use the resurrection flame to conquer your fears, conscious and subconscious. Uriel

Create Personal and Planetary Change

said you have to conquer every fear in order to achieve true God-mastery. He said:

I encourage you to take heart. For, you see, when you contemplate each fear, it is not you who are required to make it disappear. No, I say, it is the vibrant life of resurrection's flame.... When it comes to the conquering of fear, it is simply the art of letting God perform his perfect work and of you letting go.[13]

Uriel has provided an exercise to assist us. He says that there is a posture of letting go: Place your hands one over the other to your heart and then release them, opened and relaxed. Uncross your legs, breathe gently. Then speak tenderly to your soul and body: "Peace, be still." This posture reflects the serenity of the little child secure in the caring of its mother.

5. Offer devotions to your God Presence every day.

Archangel Uriel and his angels have promised to help you as you walk the path back to God's heart. They keep their promises and they will not fail to answer your call. Just prove them. Uriel says:

We have but one request of you: that you determine within your hearts to not let a day go by that you do not think upon your mighty God Presence and offer your devotions, your adorations, and your ministrations unto this mighty Source of Life. For it is through this God Presence that we are able to penetrate the darkness that is around you, that we are able to descend [to your level] and walk with you, and that you are able to ascend [to our level and be in] our presence. By this mutuality of service, this cosmic cooperation, we can move forward.[14]

Uriel says, "The Presence of God never fails! And if you will simply align yourself with this mighty force, this mighty Godpower, there can be no separation" between you and your God, you and the archangels. For it is separation from your God Reality that causes you to fail. It is separation that causes you to doubt. It is separation that causes you to fear. Uriel continues:

And I say that separation is a lie. It never existed in the mind and heart of God, and it shall not exist within you if you but heed my words this day and accept the mighty dispensations of light I have given to you!

Accept them and become one with your God Presence!... Walk the earth as Christs. Put off the old garment! Put it off and be trans-figured in the mighty transfiguring flame of life!...

All of heaven converges upon the one son of light who determines to manifest his [or her] victory. All of heaven descends to give that one the full impetus of light. It but requires the determined effort made within the heart.[15]

I hope you will come to know Archangel Uriel well enough in the depths of your being that you will make him a part of your life and daily call for his help.

URIEL *and* AURORA

RAY AND COLOR	*Sixth ray, purple and gold flecked with ruby*
QUALITIES	*Peace of God, brotherhood, ministration and service*
CHAKRA	*Solar plexus – 10 petals*
PROMINENT ON	*Thursday*
SPIRITUAL RETREAT	*Over the Tatra Mountains, south of Cracow, Poland*

ASK THEM FOR:

SPIRITUAL GIFTS	*Inner peace, tranquility of spirit*
PERSONAL ASSISTANCE WITH	*Peaceful resolution of personal, social and professional issues and relationships; creating harmony; inspiration and help for hospice workers, counselors, teachers, judges, public servants, medical professionals, and all who serve others*
HELP WITH WORLD ISSUES	*Restoring and maintaining peace, promoting brotherhood and understanding, manifesting divine justice in courtrooms and between nations*

COMMUNING *with* ANGELS *of* PEACE

AN ANGEL FROM URIEL'S BAND FOR YOU

Archangel Uriel has offered each of us an angel of his band to work with us, to help us experience the true and righteous adjudication of our souls and our affairs, and to experience the power of resurrection's flame in our personal lives and in our cities.

Call to Uriel to send one of his angels to you, and then affirm your acceptance. Your call can be as simple as this:

I call now to you, Archangel Uriel. Send to me the angel of your band that you have appointed as my helper on the sixth ray. I give my prayerful, individual assent to you and my gratitude for this gift of one of your angels to be with me:

> In the name I AM THAT I AM,
> in the name of Archangel Uriel,
> I accept the angel of the resurrection
> where I AM!

Archangel Uriel says you can repeat this affirmation over and over again as you work with the legions of the sixth ray.

Call to Uriel to settle every problem in your city. Call to him to bind and exorcise the forces of evil that perpetuate crime, poverty, bad education. After you call to Uriel's legions to pronounce God's judgment upon the forces of evil, call for the purifying of the cities with the violet flame and the resurrection flame.

THE FLAME OF THE RESURRECTION

Uriel and Aurora bear the flame of the resurrection to you. As you say the words of Jesus, "I AM the Resurrection and the Life," see this iridescent mother-of-pearl flame bringing the resurrection and the life of your service, your talent, your health, your future, your divine plan.

I AM the Resurrection and the Life!
I AM the Resurrection and the Life of
_____[name the specific situation]_____!

You can also repeat the following mantra and visualize the resurrection flame blazing through your being. Visualize it going into personal or world situations where you would send God's light.

Resurrection

I AM the flame of resurrection
Blazing God's pure light through me.
Now I AM raising every atom,
From every shadow I AM free.

I AM the light of God's full Presence,
I AM living ever free.
Now the flame of life eternal
Rises up to victory.

How Angels Help You
Create Miracles *in* Your Life

8

CHAPTER 8

ARCHANGEL ZADKIEL *and* HOLY AMETHYST

Zadkiel and Holy Amethyst are the archangel and archeia of the seventh ray. The seventh ray is the violet ray, the ray that releases the violet flame and focuses the qualities of freedom, alchemy, transformation, forgiveness and justice. It is the ray of Aquarius, the age that is at its inception and will last 2,150 years. Zadkiel explains that the violet flame is "the universal solvent that throughout the ages the alchemists have sought."[1]

Alchemists in medieval times sought to transmute base metals into gold and to discover the "elixir of life," a means for curing all diseases and securing eternal youth. The word *alchemy* is defined in a broader sense as "a power or process of transforming something common into something special" and "an inexplicable or mysterious transmuting."[2]

The highest form of alchemy is the science of self-transformation. The key to self-transformation is the violet flame. Archangel Zadkiel tells us that he possesses in his heart the secrets of alchemy. Invoke them if you will, he says, and he will release them to you.

Zadkiel is known as the angel of benevolence, mercy and memory. His name means "righteousness of God," and he teaches us the right use of the laws of God on the seventh ray. Holy Amethyst revealed that she was one of the angels who ministered to Jesus in the Garden of Gethsemane.

The seventh ray corresponds with the seat-of-the-soul chakra, which is located midway between the solar plexus and the base of the spine. This is where the soul resides in the body.

ZADKIEL *in the* SCRIPTURES

The Zohar, a key text in Kabbalah, portrays Zadkiel as one of the angels who assist Archangel Michael by carrying his banner in battle. Some traditions say that Zadkiel was the angel who restrained Abraham when he was about to sacrifice his son. In one system of the Kabbalah, Zadkiel is said to embody the fourth *sefirah*, Hesed, which is "Love," "Mercy," "Grace" or "Loving-kindness."

Zadkiel and Holy Amethyst's retreat, the Temple of Purification, is over the island of Cuba. Long ago on Atlantis, we may have visited this temple when it was physically located in the area where Cuba is today. Now it is only in the etheric octave.

In their retreat Zadkiel and Holy Amethyst prepare children of God to become priests and priestesses in the Order of Melchizedek. In the days of Atlantis both Jesus and Saint Germain studied at this retreat. Lord Zadkiel anointed them both into this priesthood. Jesus and Saint Germain set the example for us by submitting to the disciplines of the archangels in their retreats.

SAINT GERMAIN

The ascended master Saint Germain and his twin flame, Lady Master Portia, are the hierarchs of the Aquarian age. Throughout Saint Germain's past embodiments he engaged in a relentless effort to return souls of light to the worship of their Great God Source.

Saint Germain has offered us the gift of the violet flame so that we can invoke that flame, balance our karma, attain reunion with our Higher Self, and be of maximum usefulness to everyone on earth—because we will have become chalices for the violet flame.

Jesus himself taught the violet flame to his closest disciple, John the Beloved. But until the twentieth century the violet flame was not public knowledge. Now that we know about it, we can spread its teachings to the world and everyone can use it. Because Saint Germain has sponsored us and taken the responsibility for our use of it, everyone can learn to give a call to the violet flame. Try it! It will transform you and your soul forever.

VIOLET FLAME *for* RADIOACTIVITY *and the* ENVIRONMENT

Zadkiel's angels are adepts in the control of natural forces. They work with the nature spirits for the purification of earth. The nature spirits who work with the earth element are called gnomes. Those who work with the fire element and atomic energy are the salamanders. The sylphs tend the air element. And the undines look after the water element.

In recent decades an enormous amount of radioactive waste has been released into the environment. Fortunately, the violet flame can transmute these harmful radioactive elements. In fact, the violet flame is the solution to every kind of pollution. If we are going to keep our planet habitable and our genes pure, not compromised by radioactive elements, we must use the violet flame.

Saint Germain explains:

The violet flame is a physical flame!... The violet flame is closest in vibratory action of all the rays to this earth substance, to these chemical elements and compounds, to all that you see in Matter. And therefore, the violet flame can combine with any molecule or molecular structure, any particle of matter known or unknown, and any wave of light, electrons or electricity. Thus, the violet flame is the supreme antidote for food poisoning, chemical waste, toxins, pollution of drugs in the body.*

The violet flame is an elixir that you drink and imbibe like water. ... Wherever students of the ascended masters gather to invoke the violet flame, there you notice immediately an improvement in physical conditions![3]

Commit fifteen minutes a day or more to invoking the violet flame for yourself, the planet, and our future. You will see the difference in your life.

FREE YOURSELF *with the* VIOLET FLAME

Zadkiel and Holy Amethyst and their angels of purification and joy are here for one purpose and one purpose alone: to secure individual freedom with individual responsibility.

---

*In case of any such poisoning, get appropriate medical care. Take the necessary physical steps. Use the violet flame as an adjunct to your healing program.

Archangel Zadkiel says that freedom, in the ultimate sense, means access to the reservoirs of light, to the mind of God. When you are truly free because you have taken responsibility for your actions, your thoughts, your feelings, your entire life, then God grants you access to higher planes and to reservoirs of light that you can use in the service of humanity.

Zadkiel teaches, "In the fullness of God-freedom,... no thing in cosmos or in God is withheld from you."[4] The key to finding this freedom, he says, is the violet transmuting flame. "If the world today were able to accept the violet transmuting flame, most of the problems that are troubling mankind would literally melt away."[5] Archangel Zadkiel says:

How can mankind, moving among human effluvia and bric-a-brac, expect to find their freedom when their entire world resembles somewhat a great attic storehouse in which are accumulated through the ages old spinning wheels and cobwebs and crumbling mortar and brick and discordant thought?...

All of this ... imprisoned energy must find freedom by the power of the violet flame! And the mankind of earth must open the doorways of their consciousness, their chakras to expand God's light, and they must cease to give power to that which binds them and can never bring them their freedom....

The violet fire is the highest gift of God to the universe!

Zadkiel wants you to know that when you invoke this light, "millions of angels of the seventh ray do answer your call.... We see the rise, the fall, the ebb of the tide of world karma daily as the Keepers of the Flame worldwide do invoke the violet flame and therefore mitigate the effects of that mass karma."[6]

THE VIOLET FLAME WORKS WHEN YOU USE IT

The violet flame is not around us automatically. Light seeks its own level, the level of the realms of perfection, every twenty-four hours, and the violet flame does not come into our dense world unless we pull it down by exercising our throat chakra and affirming the violet flame and its action where we are. To keep yourself in that flame invoke it daily, else it will naturally gravitate back to its source. Archangel Zadkiel says:

As we see from inner levels, the tremendous effort you make to transmute the layers of your karma is truly a marvelous thing to behold. For here you sit surrounded with every kind of negative thought revolving in your aura. Then, all at once, you decide to invoke the violet flame. And lo! the mighty power of the seventh ray, as a giant electrode of cosmic energy, begins to form. And the angels gather around you. With palms outstretched they direct across your body and aura an arc of the violet ray. And as that arc flashes across your being, it vaporizes the negative conditions, and they literally disappear from heart and mind!

One of Saint Germain's students witnessed to the transforming power of the violet flame. He said, "The violet flame healed me. For years I had consulted with psychologists. They helped me to see the causes of my problems, but how could I change? Then I found the science of the spoken Word. Every day I gave violet-flame decrees. It worked! That powerful flame penetrated and dissolved core resentments that I didn't even know I had until I saw them pass into the flame, never to return. Through the violet flame I emerged healthy, vigorous and grateful! I rely on it every day."

Another student said: "Whenever I give violet flame decrees, I immediately begin to feel more centered and clear. If I have any doubts about who I am or how I am supposed to approach a difficult situation, the action of the violet flame immediately clarifies all that and helps me make the right decisions. It smooths out the wrinkles in my mind and emotions."

Zadkiel says, "Flowing with the great flow of the Holy Spirit, the violet flame frees every particle of misqualified energy that it touches."

YOUR ENERGY COLORS YOUR AURA

The energy of God that flows to you moment by moment is clear as crystal. It has no color. As soon as you send it forth, it takes on the coloration of your vibration in that moment and this shows in your aura. It could be the pure rose-pink of love. It could be yellow with illumination as you are teaching someone. It could be blue when you are calling for the will of God or have intense faith.

If you are involved with healing, music, science, the abundant life, the economy, business, or you are qualifying energy in that direction, that will increase the green in your aura. Your aura might take on the white of purity or the violet color of joy and freedom. The mother-of-pearl color of the resurrection flame shows that your energies are rising and that you are in tune with the living Christ.

Your aura, then, takes on the colorations of what you do with the energy flowing to you night and day. As long as you have life and breath, that energy is flowing to you. If you misqualify it with anything that is negative, you create karma; and that karma goes full circle, gathers more of its kind, and returns to your doorstep.

When you send out good, positive vibrations and momentums, these circle the earth, also gathering more of their kind. That good energy comes back full circle and rises to your causal body and increases the rings of light there. Whatever is the positive emphasis of your life, you increase that sphere of your causal body.

Thus the causal body is your own individual star. Saint Paul said, "One star differeth from another star in glory."[7] You have a unique causal body of light because you have uniquely sent forth energy that has come back to you and accrued to your causal body. This is the place where you have stored up your "treasures in heaven."[8]

HOW *to* BALANCE YOUR KARMA

Archangel Zadkiel and Holy Amethyst and all those who serve on the seventh ray teach us the responsibility of freedom. Yes, you are free to hate and you are free to love—but you will reap the harvest of your words and works.

Zadkiel says you cannot by a thought or "a feeling of criticism or condemnation or judgment of any individual bring one ounce of freedom to that soul or one ounce of freedom to your own."[9] Why take this grade over again in earth's schoolroom because you never get over your resentment or nonresolution? Why not reap a harvest of light and go into the next schoolroom of life?

Determine to be sincerely loving toward every part of life. When you do this, you can always find a reason to love. God dwells in every human heart. That is reason enough to love people and not to criticize and condemn them.

By using the violet flame, you can recall the negative energy you have created, which is your negative karma. Many levels of karma are recorded in the seat-of-the-soul chakra. In order to reach the point of personal Christhood and the alchemical union with the Christ, you need to balance that karma.

The violet flame is God's gift to transmute those records, to transmute the entire momentum of that negative karma, to convey a blessing to any part of life that you have ever hurt or wronged, and to send that same blessing of violet flame to those who have wronged you. This is how the violet flame helps you balance karma. The other way you balance karma is in the service you render to others, including through the job you do every day.

Don't take yourself too seriously. Five minutes from now you are going to be a different person—if you use the violet flame. So don't become overly concerned with yourself. Instead, call on the law of forgiveness. Forgiveness and mercy are the action of the violet flame. Send the violet flame to all you have ever wronged and all who have ever wronged you, and do it every day. Put all the hurts and the heartaches into the violet flame and let go! Don't take them back. Don't look at them again. Just let them go into the flame. And rejoice.

EVERY MIRACLE IS *the* FULFILLMENT *of* COSMIC LAW

Archangel Zadkiel and Holy Amethyst and the angels of the seventh ray teach us how to create miracles in our lives. People think of miracles as being beyond science. In fact, miracles are always the outpicturing of science—a science we have not probed or understood.

Every miracle that Jesus ever performed was the fulfillment of cosmic law. Jesus used the violet flame in his miracle
at Cana, where he changed water into wine. This is what Saint
Germain says about the miracle of Christ walking on the water:

*Two thousand years ago when Christ walked upon the waters
of the Sea of Galilee, his demonstration was a manifestation of the
natural law of levitation operating within an energy framework of
cohesion, adhesion, and magnetism—the very principles which make
orbital flight possible. The light atoms composing the body of Christ
absorbed at will an additional quantity of cosmic rays and spiritual
substance whose kinship to physical light made his whole body light,
thereby making it as easy for him to walk upon the sea as upon dry
land.*

*His body was purely a ray of light shining upon the waters. The
most dazzling conception of all was his ability to transfer this authority over energy to Peter through the power of Peter's own vision of the
Christ in radiant, illumined manifestation.*

*By taking his eyes temporarily from the Christ, however, Peter
entered a human fear vibration and vortex which immediately densi-
fied his body, causing it to sink partially beneath the raging seas. The
comforting hand of Christ, extended in pure love, reunited the alchemical tie; and the flow of spiritual energy through his hand raised
Peter once again to safety.*[10]

The violet flame, because it is so close to the physical vibration of our own atoms and our own bodies, is the flame and the
ray that we use for all miracles. If you begin to use the violet
flame daily, you will see what appear to be miracles in your life.

USE *the* VIOLET FLAME *for* BODY, MIND *and* SPIRIT

The violet flame can give you a physical boost. Zadkiel and Holy Amethyst say:

Why will you wait while the candle of your life burns low? You can recharge your body with the violet flame. Do you think that God is incapable of vitalizing the atoms, the cells, the molecules of your body—of flooding them with violet fire and giving you the glow of eternal youth? Do not the laws of science teach you the power within the atom itself? The violet flame has infinitely more power than a single atom. Therefore I say, Charge yourselves with this energy. Use the violet fire!

We have been walking around not realizing how heavy our bodies are as a result of the state of our human consciousness, not recognizing how light we can be and how much we can prolong our lives by giving the violet flame liberally. Saint Germain tells us some of the benefits:

For some of you, your use of the violet flame has enabled you to balance a hearty amount of karma; in others, hardness of heart has melted away from the heart chakra. You have discovered in yourself a new love, a new compassion, a new sensitivity to life, a new freedom, a new joy in pursuing that freedom. Where there has been a give and take, the violet flame has assisted in relationships with families. The violet flame has liberated you to balance old karmas, to forgive old hurts and to set you on the high road to ultimate spiritual freedom.

It is almost impossible to name all the benefits of the violet flame. Its alchemy within the personality is simply all-encompassing. The violet flame goes after the schisms that are at the root of psychological problems* that go back to earliest childhood and past lives, even those that have established such deep grooves in the record of consciousness that, for their subtlety, they have been difficult to shake lifetime after lifetime.

Archangel Zadkiel says, "The greatest step to personal progress that you can take is the consistent use of the violet transmuting flame."[11]

ZADKIEL'S FIVE KEYS *to* CREATING MIRACLES

1. Have faith in the power of the archangels to bring about change.

Let your aura be bright with faith—faith in God, faith in his Christ, faith in the fire that he has placed in your heart, faith that the angels do answer your calls. The call is always answered, even if it is not always in the way you think it should be. Zadkiel says, "Violet-flame legions of light ... can meet any condition of planet Earth. We are reinforcements ... nearest the physical octave."[12]

2. Be specific in your call.

"The world is so full with so many injustices," says Zadkiel. "Be careful that you do not waste your ammunition firing here and firing there but not making a considerable mark anywhere."[13] Instead, examine the world scene and choose your cause or the causes that are worth fighting for. Choose one or

---

The violet flame, while effective in dealing with psychological problems, is not a replacement for professional advice. The violet flame is an adjunct and a facilitator.

two causes, and then work on them relentlessly with your decrees, your meditation.

Actively participate in any kind of group that has set its course on that same cause, and decree on that situation. Band together with the wonderful people who are working on that cause but who do not know the power and the science of decrees. See how things will happen because you are contributing what you know how best to do, which is to call forth the violet flame.

3. Send missiles of violet flame.

Zadkiel says: In answer to your call we send "missiles of violet flame ... spiritual rockets of compressed violet fire—compressed to such an intensity" as to consume layers and layers of records of the evil works of fallen angels. It takes a serious commitment and daily self-discipline so that in the hour of need you are prayed up. You can call for these missiles of violet fire to penetrate the physical body of the earth and to save the people. "With God all things are possible!"[14]

4. Saturate your aura with violet flame.

Think of your aura as a violet-flame fountain, that all whom you meet can come and drink of that fountain of light. Always have violet flame stored up and present with you, available for someone in need.

Zadkiel says, "To make the difference in world prophecy the violet flame must pass through from our octave into the physical through you, through your auras and your chakras" to the people who need it. "A truth has never been more true—that Divine Intercession must become physical through the saints in embodiment."[15]

Adepts of all ages have used the alchemy of the violet flame to accomplish the healings and miracles, prophecies and judgments that were the very signs of their coming. The saturation of their auras by the violet flame was and is the means whereby the avatars have held the balance of world karma. By the amplification of the violet flame through the seat-of-the-soul chakra, they have engaged in planetary trans-mutation of darkness by light and they have survived as pillars of fire midst the planetary weight of evil.

World karma is very heavy in these days. We see plagues coming upon the earth. Life is more difficult. The economy is difficult. Jobs are difficult. It seems to take greater effort to get anything done. Everything we do today, we really have to work hard for. That is why we need the violet flame.

5. The key to change is to get involved.
Zadkiel says that the open door to light in the physical octave is you and is in the power of your spoken Word to decree, to demonstrate, and to protest any and all injustices in your community. You are the open door through which the violet flame comes to earth. "Pray at the altar, then go forth and take your stand in all areas where life is threatened. You are the open door to safety and salvation in the earth."[16]

Invite the archangels and their legions into your life and into the life of every nation, naming the specific issues—because unless you name the issues, the situations, the circum-stances in your life where you want angelic intercession, the angels will not answer you specifically.

Make a list of the top twenty-five problems you see on planet Earth and assign the angels daily in God's name to solve those problems. Try the angels and see how they can make the difference in your life.

ZADKIEL *and* HOLY AMETHYST

RAY AND COLOR	*Seventh ray, violet*
QUALITIES	*Freedom, alchemy, transmutation, forgiveness and justice*
CHAKRA	*Seat of the soul – 6 petals*
PROMINENT ON	*Saturday*
SPIRITUAL RETREAT	*Over the island of Cuba*

ASK THEM FOR:

SPIRITUAL GIFTS	*Soul freedom, happiness, joy, forgiveness, justice, mercy, dissolution of painful memories and negative traits, self-transformation*
PERSONAL ASSISTANCE WITH	*Tolerance, diplomacy, learning how to forgive*
HELP WITH WORLD ISSUES	*Dissolution of memories of strife between nations and ethnic groups; inspiration for the creative negotiation and writing of laws, regulations, fiscal and economic policies, trade and peace agreements*

COMMUNING *with* ANGELS *of the* VIOLET FLAME

When you call to Zadkiel and Holy Amethyst, they will saturate you, your mind, your feelings, your thoughts, your heart, your soul, your chakras with the violet flame. Visualize violet flame swirling around your chakras. Making the call can be as simple as this:

> Archangel Zadkiel and Holy Amethyst, help me
> this day to _____.

Fill in the blank, telling them what you need help with. Ask them and their angels to go to trouble spots in the world where people are suffering and to give them the violet flame.

Consciously direct violet flame into any and every problem in your life, small and great. No problem is too insignificant to pray about and no problem is so big that it is unsolvable—so name them all.

VIOLET FLAME CHAKRA CLEARANCE

The way to balance karma and balance relationships is to balance your own chakras. And to balance your chakras, you simply must use the violet flame. The violet flame is essential to use because it will clear all seven levels and planes of your being and balance your karma.

I invite you to try it. Use the violet flame daily for six months and call to Saint Germain and the archangels. You will find such a change in your life, your consciousness, your ability to think and function and to know who you are that you will simply be amazed.

For this chakra clearance, we begin with the heart chakra and move in a spiral above and below the heart. We use this order because we want to duplicate the spiral of the causal body that is above, here below. See the violet flame blazing through the debris and substance that it is consuming as you give each affirmation. Say each set three times.

My heart is a chakra of violet fire,
My heart is the purity God desires!

I AM a being of violet fire,
I AM the purity God desires!

My throat chakra is a wheel of violet fire,
My throat chakra is the purity God desires!

I AM a being of violet fire,
I AM the purity God desires!

My solar plexus is a sun of violet fire,
My solar plexus is the purity God desires!

I AM a being of violet fire,
I AM the purity God desires!

My third eye is a center of violet fire,
My third eye is the purity God desires!

I AM a being of violet fire,
I AM the purity God desires!

My soul chakra is a sphere of violet fire,
My soul is the purity God desires!

I AM a being of violet fire,
I AM the purity God desires!

My crown chakra is a lotus of violet fire,
My crown chakra is the purity God desires!

I AM a being of violet fire,
I AM the purity God desires!

My base chakra is a fount of violet fire,
My base chakra is the purity God desires!

I AM a being of violet fire,
I AM the purity God desires!

When you give the concluding verse, see this whole spiral that starts from the heart becoming a whirling disc of violet flame. By that whirling action it becomes a magnet pulling down the light of the Father, raising the light of the Mother within you.

VIOLET FLAME AFFIRMATIONS

As you give the following affirmation, remember that the words "I AM" are the name of God, your Mighty I AM Presence. When you say "I AM the violet flame in action in me now," you really mean "God in me is the violet flame in action in me now." The flame is God, and it is God who sends forth the violet flame so that we can use it. God is in action in us. When you affirm this, you are affirming the totality of your being as manifesting the action of God's violet flame.

I AM the Violet Flame

I AM the violet flame
   In action in me now
I AM the violet flame
   To light alone I bow
I AM the violet flame
   In mighty cosmic power
I AM the light of God
   Shining every hour
I AM the violet flame
   Blazing like a sun
I AM God's sacred power
   Freeing every one

How *to* Meet
Your Guardian Angel

9

HOW *to* MEET YOUR GUARDIAN ANGEL

*Y*our guardian angel already knows you better than anyone else in the universe, and that is why he or she is your guardian and your friend. Your chief guardian angel is none other than your Holy Christ Self.

How did your Holy Christ Self come to be known as your guardian angel? This is because in the two thousand years since the coming of Jesus Christ we have not been taught that we each have a Christ Presence. Therefore people came to acknowledge that presence, that friend and guide, as their personal angel. And indeed your Holy Christ Self *is* your personal angel.

The seven archangels may send other guardian angels to you from time to time. Depending on your devotion and love and the number of assignments you give them, you may have dozens of guardian angels who answer your prayers and help loved ones. Your Holy Christ Self, your chief guardian angel, is the one who directs them.

Our Christ Self is our Real Self. The fact that we have a Holy Christ Self is not merely a Christian concept. Jeremiah prophesied the coming of the Real Self, whom he called The Lord Our Righteousness, a fitting name for the Holy Christ Self. *Righteousness* means the *right use* of God's laws. We need to be educated in God's laws to be certain that everything we ask of our angels is lawful, and this is what our Christ Presence, our guardian angel, teaches us. This Real Self is also known as the Higher Self or Higher Consciousness.

Your Holy Christ Self, the real you, is who you were when God created you and your twin flame out of his white-fire body, the original causal body—the Body of First Cause.* By and by, after aeons of experiencing perfection in this Great Causal Body of God, you elected by the exercise of free will to depart from that perfection and explore the denser spheres of the matter universe.

This is when you and your twin flame began to make karma, specifically negative karma. The law of karma then caused you to be tied to the realms of imperfection where you made that karma. This is why we are all here. This is why we have partial knowledge of who we are and where we have come from. And this is why God has sent his angels to remind us, to quicken our ancient memory of who we are and where we came from.

We are wearing mortal bodies in place of the immortal bodies we once wore, and we are *not* face to face with our God. We are human in so very many ways. But we are also divine, and it is the divinity in us that beholds God face to face. The essence of our divinity, our Holy Christ Self, *does* see God, our Mighty I AM Presence, and does reflect that Divine Image back upon

---

There is a causal body in the Great Central Sun, and there is an individual replica of that causal body above you surrounding your I AM Presence.

our souls so that we might daily start to put on, once again, the image and likeness of God in which we were originally made.

The Gospel of Matthew gives Jesus' teaching on this angel beholding the face of the Father: "Take heed that ye despise not one of these little ones; for I say unto you, That in heaven their angels do always behold the face of my Father which is in heaven."[1]

GNOSTIC BELIEFS ABOUT ANGELS

Some early Christians, known as gnostics, had a unique belief about angels. The gnostics were members of early Christian sects who believed that they possessed the secret, or mystical, teachings of Jesus and that this special knowledge was the means to salvation. Some gnostic writings teach that the spiritual counterpart of the gnostic is an angel. In other words, they also called the Holy Christ Self an angel.

The goal of the gnostic is to become the bride of his angel. The gnostic teacher Heracleon calls this angelic counterpart the *husband* of the gnostic.[2] To the soul, who abides in the human body, the gnostics assigned the feminine gender and referred to the soul as *she*. And to the angel, or Holy Christ Self, they assigned the masculine gender.

In the mystical tradition of Catholicism, the soul is seeking to become the bride of Jesus Christ. Even some non-Catholics believe this. Aimee Semple McPherson, the great Christian evangelist of the twentieth century, published a magazine called *Bridal Call*. She was always waiting for the Bridegroom to come and receive her soul. So this concept of being the bride of Christ has figured for two thousand years in Christian thinking. In other traditions this bonding is called the alchemical marriage.

The ascended masters teach that our soul is intended to be wed, or bonded, to our own Holy Christ Self. We were bonded with him in the beginning, but we lost that bonding. It is as though the Bridegroom had divorced us because we were no longer in the pure vibration of divine love.

The way to achieve this bonding again is by giving devotion to God and by giving love in every possible circumstance, withstanding any temptation to anger. By practicing the presence of Christ and by walking in his footsteps and striving daily to be bonded once again with our Lord, we seek to be restored to our First Estate, where we were when God created us.

GUARDIAN ANGELS AROUND *the* WORLD

Some of the world's religions teach that God assigns each of us a guardian angel, whose job is to watch over and care for us. The Hebrews and some early Christians also taught that nations had their own guardian angels. These angels, they believed, could guard the nation and plead for it when it was threatened by divine punishment.

Islam teaches that each person has four guardian angels who protect him against evil forces. Two angels guard a person during the day and two at night. According to Islamic teaching, the guardian angel stationed to the right of a man writes down his good works immediately. The angel at his left records his evil deeds a few hours after he commits them, first giving him some time to repent.

The Catholic Church teaches that each of the faithful has his own guardian angel. They believe your guardian angel assists you in your spiritual, bodily and earthly affairs, as these pertain to your salvation. Catholic tradition explains the role of guardian angels as twofold. First, they protect and direct man. Saint Basil said: "It is a teaching of Moses that every believer has an Angel to guide him as a teacher and a shepherd."[3]

Second, guardian angels act as intercessors. Catholics are encouraged to ask the angels to pray for them and to protect them. If you were raised as a Catholic, you might remember this prayer:

> *Angel of God, my guardian dear,*
> *To whom God's love commits me here,*
> *Ever this day, be at my side*
> *To light and guard, to rule and guide. Amen.*

Saint Bernard urged reverence for guardian angels:

Always remember that you are in the presence of your Guardian Angel....

If we truly love our Guardian Angel, we cannot fail to have boundless confidence in his powerful intercession with God and firm faith in his willingness to help us. This will inspire us frequently to invoke his aid and protection, especially in time of temptation and trial. It will prompt us also to ask his counsel in the many problems which confront us, in matters both great and small. Many of the saints made it a practice never to undertake anything without first seeking advice of their Guardian Angel.[4]

Indeed, our Holy Christ Self is our counselor and our adviser.

WALK *and* TALK *with* YOUR GUARDIAN ANGEL

The third-century Church theologian Origen of Alexandria taught that the angel who attends you will withdraw if by disobedience you become unworthy. Saint Jerome taught that you can drive away your guardian angel when you do not repent of your sins. Saint Basil said: "Sin turns away angels as smoke turns away bees and a nasty stench puts to flight doves."[5]

It is not that God is punishing us or that our guardian angels would desert us. It is that by our being out of alignment with God's will we have put a great vibrational distance between ourselves and the angels.

Origen also cites the teaching given in early Christian texts that good and bad angels influence the thoughts and actions of men. The Jewish philosopher Philo contends that within each soul there lives a good angel and a wicked angel. *The Shepherd of Hermas*, a text held in high regard by early Christians, says:

There are two angels with man; one of righteousness, the other of iniquity....

The angel of righteousness is mild and modest and gentle and quiet. When therefore, he gets into thy heart, immediately he talks with thee of righteousness, of modesty, of chastity, of bountifulness of forgiveness, of charity, and piety.

When all these things come into thy heart, know then that the angel of righteousness is with thee.... Hearken to this angel and to his works....

When anger overtakes thee, or bitterness, know that [the angel of iniquity] is in thee.[6]

If you really want to walk and talk with your guardian angel, there is nothing to stop you. No barrier will be set up by your angel. The only barrier is perhaps your shyness or fear or forgetfulness in speaking to God, confessing your sins, telling him you desire to do better and to live a life that fits you for your goal of union with him.

Starting a new life with not only your guardian angel but all of the angels of heaven is just as easy as turning around and walking into a room. Remember that God made the angels to be our caregivers all the way Home.

SAINTS, POPES *and* THEIR GUARDIAN ANGELS

Saint Francis de Sales was very devoted to guardian angels. Before beginning his sermons he would always ask the guardian angels of his congregation to open the people's hearts to his message. Author Gloria Gibson writes that Saint Francis de Sales "used to send messages to friends by giving them to his guardian angel, who immediately transferred them to that friend's guardian angel."[7]

Pope Pius XI was also devoted to his guardian angel. Author George Huber says that Pope Pius encouraged the future Pope John XXIII, then a monsignor and apostolic delegate, to express a similar devotion. Pius said to the future Pope John:

> *Whenever we have to speak with someone who is rather closed to our argument and with whom therefore the conversation needs to be very persuasive, we go to our guardian angel. We ask our angel to take it up with the guardian angel of the person we have to see. And once the two angels establish an understanding, the Pope's conversation is much easier.*[8]

Pope John XXIII considered devotion to guardian angels an essential part of one's spiritual life. He once said that it was through his guardian angel that God inspired him to convoke his landmark ecumenical council. When Pope John addressed a crowd, he would imagine the guardian angels of those present and send them a silent greeting. He wrote to his niece, "It is consoling to feel this special guardian near us, this guide of our steps, this witness of our most intimate actions." He also said that our guardian angel "is a good adviser who intercedes near God, on our behalf, who helps us in our needs, who protects us from dangers and accidents."[9] "Get to know him. Talk to him. He will answer you."[10]

ENCOUNTERS *with* GUARDIAN ANGELS

I received a letter from a woman telling me of a cherished experience of oneness with her Holy Christ Self. She wrote:

In my thirty-eighth year, I had an amazing experience. I was sitting in my living room caring for our newest arrival, when suddenly a powerfully uplifting light and radiation began to fill my outer awareness. It continued for several days. I praised and thanked God and asked to understand more perfectly this wonderful blessing.

After a few days of this, I suddenly realized that the vibration of this light was that of the Christ consciousness entering my being. I called to my Christ Self and it intensified. I knew that I could now see and feel more clearly what the Christ flame really was and how to better call it forth minute by minute. It became real for me in a much deeper way.

Before this point, I hadn't consciously experienced the mantle of my Christ Self and did not know what it might feel like. Now almost every waking moment I was concentrating on affirming the living Christ within me and calling forth my beloved Holy Christ Self....

I wanted that relationship that I believe many mystics of the Christian dispensation had with Jesus. Now a door is opening and I can see a real possibility of this within my own heart!

Another woman recounted an experience with her guardian angel and Archangel Michael:

I was about ten or eleven years old. It was a hot summer day and my father had just picked up my sister and me from our summer camp and we were driving home. I was exhausted and sleepy—so sleepy that I thought it would be wonderful to lean my head up against the car door and fall asleep. As I was about to do this, a strange yet beautiful thing happened.

I heard a voice. I shall never forget that voice. It was a female voice—firm yet gentle, commanding yet soothing. The voice spoke to me and said: "No, do not lay down your head. Wait until you get home."

I do not have the words to describe the beauty of this voice nor the depth of this being's care for me. Such is an angel's love. I instantly obeyed her command and raised myself to a more upright position.

Shortly thereafter—seconds or minutes—our car was hit broadside by another car and the side on which I was sitting was completely smashed in. If I had laid my head down as I had intended, I might have incurred severe head injuries and perhaps died. My gratitude to God for the wondrous intercession and devotion of the angels of Light!

Your guardian angel knows you very well. The seven archangels will send other guardian angels to you if you need them, so by your devotions you may have more than one guardian angel who is taking care of you, your family and loved ones, your neighborhood, your town or city, your country and the world.

COMMUNING *with* YOUR GUARDIAN ANGEL

HOW TO CALL TO YOUR GUARDIAN ANGEL

A call to your guardian angel can be as simple as this:

Dear God, send my guardian angel to me now.

This is a simple prayer and a request, and believe it or not, this is all that's needed. You can then offer other prayers to God on behalf of loved ones and for very specific needs.

PRAYER TO YOUR GUARDIAN ANGEL

One way to meet your guardian angel is by praying to him or her. The following prayer is a vehicle you can use to express your devotion to God and your chief guardian angel, your Holy Christ Self. The words are a vessel into which you pour your love. Let the words lead you to the restoration of the consciousness of God that you had in the beginning.

You can also use this prayer to direct your love to Chamuel and Charity, the archangels who are the guardians of your physical heart, your heart chakra, and of the threefold flame, the divine spark in your heart. This flame is called "threefold" because it engenders the primary attributes of the Trinity—power, wisdom and love.

Prayer to Your Chief Guardian Angel

1. Holy Christ Self above me,
   Thou balance of my soul,

Let thy blessed radiance
Descend and make me whole.

Refrain: Thy flame within me ever blazes,
Thy peace about me ever raises,
Thy love protects and holds me,
Thy dazzling light enfolds me.
I AM thy threefold radiance,
I AM thy living Presence
Expanding, expanding, expanding now.

2. Holy Christ Flame within me,
Come, expand thy triune light;
Flood my being with the essence
Of the pink, blue, gold and white.

3. Holy lifeline to my Presence,
Friend and brother ever dear,
Let me keep thy holy vigil,
Be thyself in action here.

In giving this devotion you have begun to reconnect
with all the divine love you knew in the beginning with God
and your twin flame. Your Holy Christ Self as your chief
guardian angel is not only the mediator of your soul's union
with God but is also the mediator of your soul's union with
your twin flame.

A VERY PERSONAL PRAYER

Here is a very personal prayer to your guardian angel and his or her flame within you, the Holy Christ Flame. In the first verse you are speaking to your guardian angel, and in the second verse your guardian angel is answering you.

Prayer to the Holy Christ Flame

Thou Holy Christ Flame within my heart
Help me to manifest all thou art
Teach me to see thyself in all
Help me to show men how to call
All of thy glory from the Sun
'Til earth's great victory is won
I AM we love thee, thou art our all!
I AM we love thee, hear our call!

I hear thy call, my children dear
I AM thy heart, so never fear
I AM your mind, your body, too
I AM in every cell of you.
I AM thy earth and sea and sky
And not one soul shall I pass by
I AM in thee, thou art in me
I AM, I AM thy victory.

When you give this prayer, you are talking to your guardian angel, renewing the tie. It is so important to do so, and you can pray to your guardian angel at any moment or hour of the day. It doesn't have to be formal. Just keep the channels of communication open and you will see how each day you will have a greater sensitivity to that presence who is with you always.

You can read these words and know that this is the comfort that your guardian angel is speaking to you. Eventually, you can develop a listening ear and heart, learn to screen out the voices of the world, and hear your Holy Christ Self speaking to you directly.

How *to* Work *with*
Angels *for* Success

10

HOLY JUSTINIUS *and the* BANDS *of* SERAPHIM

Holy Justinius is the Captain of Seraphic Bands. He is the head of the order of angels known as the seraphim. The name Justinius means "he who is just."

The word *seraphim* is derived from the Hebrew verb meaning "to consume with fire" or "to burn." In some traditions, the seraphim are called the "burning ones." But the root of the word *seraphim* is an active verb; thus, rather than meaning they are "ardent or glowing beings," the seraphim should be seen as agents of purification by fire. The seraphim depicted in Christian art are often painted red, symbolizing fire. In fact, they do not have hot red flames around them but the cool white flames of God's purification.

In Jewish lore and Christian theology, seraphim are the highest order of angels. According to tradition, seraphim are ministering servants who surround the throne of God and perpetually sing, "Holy, holy, holy, Lord God Almighty." As they continually intone this mantra, they embody the holiness of God.

Seraphim are perpetually absorbed in love and adoration

of God. They are also in adoration of God as Mother, and they compose the honor guard of all who represent the Divine Mother.

Holy Justinius teaches that the seraphim are fiery beings who form concentric rings round the Central Sun. As they make their rounds they absorb the light and fire of the Central Sun and they come to earth and the far-flung planets truly trailing clouds of glory, processioning down the highways of cosmos.[1] Justinius says:

> *Seraphim, angelic beings, are mighty in height, for you see, they are accustomed to the dimensions of other worlds. And as they stand before the altar of the sacred fire they [appear as] flames that spiral ever higher....*
>
> *If you could penetrate the paintings of Gustave Doré of angelic scenes across the cosmos, you would see that even the suggestion from the pen of the artist of an infinite multitude of heavenly hosts cannot even begin to show how cosmos is packed with the beings of light, of cherubim and seraphim.[2]*

Justinius says, "Untold millions of seraphim are in my command."[3] If you want the help of seraphim, call to their captain. You can simply say, "Hail, Justinius, Captain of Seraphic Bands! Send seraphim to guard my house, my children, my community, my planet, my nation."

The more you walk a path of your own personal Christhood, the more you will be respected by angels and the more they will cluster around you. The more you send out divine love and desire to help many, the more they will strengthen you.

ENCOUNTERS *with the* SERAPHIM

There is a Jewish text called *The Life of Adam and Eve*, in which a six-winged seraph carries Adam to the Lake of Acheron and washes him three times in God's presence. Remember that we are all sons and daughters of God, and so what one son or daughter of God has been blessed with, we may also be blessed with. If you would like a six-winged seraph to cleanse and wash you three times, call for this in the name of the Father, the Son and the Holy Spirit and see what God's will is for you.

The Third Book of Enoch is an apocryphal work that records this teaching on the seraphim:

How many seraphim are there? Four, corresponding to the four winds of the world. How many wings have each of them? Six, corresponding to the six days of creation. How many faces have they? Sixteen, four facing in each direction. The measure of the seraphim and the height of each of them corresponds to the seven heavens. The size of each wing is as the fullness of a heaven, and the size of each face is like the rising sun. Every one of them radiates light like the splendor of the throne of glory, so that even the holy creatures, the majestic ophanim, and the glorious cherubim cannot look on that light, for the eyes of anyone who looks on it grow dim from its great brilliance.[4]

The only biblical reference to the seraphim is in the Book of Isaiah:

In the year that king Uzziah died, I saw also the Lord sitting upon a throne, high and lifted up, and his train filled the temple. Above it stood the seraphims: each one had six wings; with two he covered his face, and with two he covered his feet, and with two he did fly.

And one cried unto another, and said, Holy, holy, holy, is the LORD of hosts: the whole earth is full of his glory.

And the posts of the door moved at the voice of him that cried, and the house was filled with smoke.

Then said I, Woe is me! for I am undone; because I am a man of unclean lips, and I dwell in the midst of a people of unclean lips: for mine eyes have seen the King, the LORD of hosts.

Then flew one of the seraphims unto me, having a live coal in his hand, which he had taken with the tongs from off the altar:

And he laid it upon my mouth, and said, Lo, this hath touched thy lips; and thine iniquity is taken away, and thy sin purged.

Also I heard the voice of the Lord, saying: Whom shall I send, and who will go for us? Then said I, Here am I; send me.[5]

It's wonderful to wait upon the LORD and it is a great moment in eternity when the LORD sends forth the call to you. The next greatest moment in eternity is when you answer that call, saying, "Here am I, send me!"

The angel of the LORD has commissioned each and every one of you at some point in your life, perhaps in the deepest recesses of your soul, perhaps in a memory that is too far back to quite quicken. But you have been called to whatever you are to do in this life as surely as Isaiah was called for his mission.

Saint Francis of Assisi, in the later years of his life, had an ecstatic vision of a seraph nailed to a cross. One of his biographers recounts the episode:

While he was in a state of ecstasy with God one morning, as he was praying on a slope of the mountain, lo, he beheld a seraph with six wings, resplendent with fire, descend from the heights of Heaven.

When with his exceedingly swift flight he arrived in the air at a point near the man of God, the image of a crucified man appeared behind the wings. Two wings rose above the head, two others were spread as though poised in flight, and the last two entirely hid the body.

At the sight of the vision, the servant of Christ was struck with a sense of wonderment and his heart was suffused with a joy mixed with pain.... Upon disappearing, the vision left a prodigious ardor in his heart and imprinted upon his flesh marks no less prodigious. Indeed, soon thereafter the signs of nails, as he had seen them an instant before on that image of the crucified man, began to appear on his hands and feet. On his right side, he had the red scar of a wound as though he had been pierced by a lance.[6]

MY ENCOUNTER *with the* SERAPHIM

My college apartment in Boston was just a couple of blocks away from the Christian Science Mother Church. Late one evening I was praying for a loved one who was ill and I had the impulse to walk to the church. I desired healing so much for this person that I said to God in my heart, "I know that if I will just put my hands on the walls of this wonderful church, I will be able to transfer that healing light to this one."

No one was around the church. I approached the first set of large doors and I put my hands on the wall beside them. As soon as I did this I saw huge fiery angels, one on each side of the entrance, guarding the doors of the church.

This was such an extraordinary experience that something in me wanted to say, "This isn't real. This is not happening." And yet I saw it. So I said to myself, "Well, I'll try the next set of doors."

This is a very large church; it seats more than three

thousand people. I ran around to the next set of doors, I put my hands on the walls, and there were the seraphim. I went around to all the doors of the church. There were seraphim at every door.

Although Mary Baker Eddy taught that angels were real beings, that particular teaching is ignored in the Christian Science Church. Their standard interpretation is that "angels are God's thoughts passing to man."[7] In other words, angels are just ideas.

This was an amazing thing. Here was a group of people who in their metaphysics do not believe in angels as tangible beings, and yet angels are guarding their church.

That vision was a tremendous moment in my life and I was filled with light. I went back to my apartment and I put my hands on the one who was sick, and he was well. And I thought in my heart, "Is there any end to the glorious opportunities of serving God and knowing his angels?"

PARTNER *with* ANGELS *for* SUCCESS

Success means we have done something well—we have achieved or accomplished a goal, we have done a good job. In our society success usually means that we have a good income, we are happy, and we are leading a good life. Yet how many times have you seen successful people who are so tied up with the materialistic success of their lives that they have not even considered that they can be successful spiritually or be a failure spiritually?

I think success starts with getting yourself aligned with the blueprint of the will of God for you in the beginning. Success is becoming who you really are. You can have all the success in the world that you want; there's nothing wrong with this—

Jesus promised the abundant life. But there is a foundation that is necessary for lasting success and lasting fulfillment.

Success really begins with the decision to live a life in God, through God, for God and for his people—rather than to live for yourself, only to take what everything and everybody can do for you. Lasting success goes beyond this life, beyond the few short decades you have in this body. It is a success whereby you increase the rings on your tree of life by quality living, quality experience with others and in God.

Be willing to listen to the voice of God within and to cultivate that voice. This voice is your conscience. It is your Higher Self. Many people do not hear the voice of God because they have long ago silenced that voice. They do not want to hear what it has to say, because then they might have to do something they do not want to do.

Each lifetime is a pyramid and you are building the foundation each time you take a right step, because you have listened to God and followed his will. I have found in my life that if I ever skipped one direction from God I would miss a whole chain, because each direction and my fulfillment of it led to the next and the next.

When you do not have wholeness, your fragmented self compromises the alchemy of your life—the steps you take to bring change to yourself or the world around you. When you are right with God, everything you touch will be successful.

Being right with God means you really do have to work on your psychology. Read books on psychology. Work with a therapist if necessary. Heal the separated parts of yourself with God's help and the help of seraphim. The angels will teach you to be successful and they will work with you for success.

SET GOALS *and* WRITE DOWN YOUR PLAN

When you have a plan, you are more likely to bring into manifestation precisely what you want. Set goals for yourself—what you want to accomplish from this day forward for the rest of your life. Meditate on them, write them down. Your plan can be a list of statements about what is going to happen in your life and what you are willing to do to make it happen, or it can take the form of a treasure map.

Pick a reasonable age to which you think you will live and then ask, "What can I realistically accomplish?" Cross out about nine-tenths of the things that you think you might do or even will do. Concentrate on a definite purpose that you know will leave this world a better place.

Discover what your divine plan is for this life. If you don't, you could be wasting a lifetime. Only you can know what that plan is. You discover it in your heart. Pray to God to reveal it to you. Then work hard, educate yourself, and get into a position where you can have the material things that you need and want in life and that support you in fulfilling your divine plan.

Always dedicate your efforts to God. Offer him a tenth of what you receive, as Abraham offered a tenth of the spoils of battle to Melchizedek.[8] If you do not know of a church to which you want to tithe, give to the best charity you know or to some good cause that you know will help people.

It is so important to remember that a tenth of what you have belongs to God. It is the yeast that multiplies the rest! When you give God a tenth, he uses it as a leaven and gives back to you a hundred percent each time. It is unfailing. When you tithe you multiply your abundance.

JOIN *the* ANGELS *of* VICTORY

Once you have established a major goal and written down the means by which you are going to achieve that goal, the angels of Victory will help you hold on to your sense of victory and determination. The angels of Victory are fierce and have a tremendous determination—and they will infuse *you* with that God-determination.

Your life goal will always have in it something for you, something for your family, something for humanity. You need to be enriched spiritually, intellectually and in every way by what you are doing—and the rest of the world can be too. It is a great joy to see that something you have done has helped people.

Mighty Victory, an ascended master who has been devoted to the flame of victory for thousands of years, says that the only time anyone can take from you your victory is when you lose the sense of victory and when you fail to claim your victory.[9] You may have a victory but the fallen angels will never, never admit it. You have to claim that victory even after you have won it and affirm that it is yours and that no one can take it from you.

"It takes more than proximity! It takes *appropriation*," says Mighty Victory. In other words, you cannot just warm yourself by the fires of his legions. You must *become* the spirit of victory. Be the flame of victory, the mood of victory, the joy and the momentum of victory.[10]

How do you do this? Write yourself signs. Put them on the wall, put them on the mirror or wherever you will see them. Remind yourself that you have twenty-four hours in that day and you better be up and doing something to accomplish the

goal of your life. Banish from your mind any sense of defeatism. Take care of your subconscious and unconscious so you do not have negativity popping up just when you are about to achieve your victory.

Angels of Victory will help you overcome self-belittlement and pessimism. We have probably all had the experience at one time or another where all of a sudden we get the idea that we just cannot achieve what we have set as our goal. But we *can* do it if we have been realistic. That's why the word *realism* is so important to us today—it's because many people do not want to see reality.

Mighty Victory tells us, "Remove from your mind and consciousness tonight that you are a deficient person, and enter instead into the consciousness that you are an efficient, God-free being determined to embark upon the course of your own cosmic victory."[11]

Have patience with yourself and others. Avoid criticizing them and you will avoid the returning karma of others criticizing you and weighing you down. One of the major things that could stand between you and your union with God in this life is your failure to transmute your condemnation of yourself or any part of life. Mighty Victory tells us, "Remember well the words of Christ, 'Inasmuch as ye have done it unto one of the least of these my brethren, ye have done it unto me.' Take, then, the mystery of victory. All humanity who stand before you are gods in disguise.... [They are] potentials of Christhood."[12]

THE ANGELS ARE READY *to* HELP

One of the most important things in goal-fittedness is to be a disciple of Jesus or Gautama or of someone who is a great teacher of the past or the present. Being a disciple means being disciplined on the Path. Then, have a sense of humor and greet your challenges with joy. You get pretty seasoned after a while.

The challenges of life will come your way with regularity. I used to be very concerned and bowed down by them. Then one day I finally realized that I had not gone through a single crisis in my entire life where God did not deliver me by his angels. So I said to myself, "You are not going to let any crisis move you at all ever again, because you know the outcome— God is going to save you when your cause is just."

Instead of being bowed down by life's challenges, go to the altar and pray. Pray without ceasing. Give the calls to God and empower the angels to deliver you, and they will. It is such a freedom when you are absolutely determined that nothing is going to take your success from you, no matter what, because God has willed it. It is an amazing thing to no longer be moved by those voices that tell you some terrible calamity is coming upon you. Be free today from the fear that anything can come near you that could destroy you. Do not believe it. God is in you and his angels are ready to help you.

How have we ever convinced ourselves that we are some lowly creatures? That's the work of the fallen angels. Taste your victory, smell your victory, imbibe your victory, be your victory!

CLAIM YOUR VICTORY

Prepare for your spiritual tests, for they are coming. You cannot just slide into an exam without preparation; you need to know the facts, know what spiritual laws you can invoke in your defense. Your Higher Self is your advocate, and you also have to be your own advocate, so be careful not to waste time, money or energy.

When you are feeling low, instantly call to the angels of Victory. Mighty Victory says, "One fiat by which I invoke the angels" is "'The earth is the Lord's and the fullness thereof.'"[13]

Build a momentum of victory. Every time you have a victory, write it down. Read back to yourself all the victories you have achieved in this life—in spite of every kind of adversity, including your own karma. When you have a momentum on achieving victories, you set yourself up for victories, not failures.

The fallen angels are not going to give you your victory. They are not going to give you the earth or even the seat you are sitting on. They will try to take everything you have from you. So you have to seize the torch of your victory, and sometimes you have to wrest it from those rebel angels who are trying to take it away from you.

You also have to defend your victory. Sometimes you have to be *very* bold and outspoken so that nobody can come along and steal your victory, steal your invention, steal your project, your best friend or your family.

There are many success courses that have a lot of good to teach us. You can always learn from successful people, and many successful people are writing good books. All you have to do is take the teachings of the angels, the decrees and the violet flame and combine the spiritual path with what has made people in America successful.

Whether you study Dale Carnegie or Napoleon Hill or

more recent motivational speakers, there are formulas for success that you can follow step by step as taught. And remember, the only lasting success comes when you take those principles and put them on the foundation of the rock of your own personal Christhood. Decide once and for all that you *can* trust God, you *can* trust your Inner Self and you *can* win.

THE PATH *to* REUNION *with* GOD

The seraphim are here to help you achieve the ultimate success—your successful reunion with God in the ritual of the ascension. Justinius says, "I ask for you to consider this goal for yourself, the goal of the ascension, and not to postpone it to another lifetime or some undefined future. The ascension is this day."

Think about how you are attaining union with God moment by moment. Molecule by molecule of thought, of heart, of feeling, you are entering into that grand union. Every day a part of you is ascending back to God.

Why desire this? Not for ambition, not to have power over others. Desire union with God for only one reason—so that you will have an empowerment to help other people, to serve to set all life free, to heal this planet, so that you can do something about mankind's problems.

That is the reason to seek God—not to escape, not to be pious before men, not to be different in any way, but because you want that oneness with God that was experienced by the saints who did their job, did it well, and didn't seek any acclaim. Some of them were not even noticed and their names have not been written down in history, and yet they have been the pillars of fire in the earth. They were always accompanied by seraphim, and you can be too.

You *can* meet the seraphim. You may see them or you may not. Either way, you can know this for a certainty: They are present. So rejoice in their presence and rejoice in your opportunity to come nearer to God through his holy angels.

Holiness is not some kind of antiseptic state. It is not rigidity. It is not a robot mentality where you try to be humanly perfect. There is no such thing as human perfection; that is a misnomer. All humans are imperfect. But that is not what God is looking at.

God is looking at your heart, at your soul, at your mind. God is looking in the very depths of your being—the desire of your heart, the bent of your life, the direction you are taking. Do you contribute light to the world, helping to ignite a flame in each one whom you meet, able to lend your light to them because you never let your own oil run out, because you keep your chakras brimming with light so you have always something to give?

The way of the angels and the way of the ascended masters is doable. It is practical. It is a mystical path, a path you walk with God. And you have the intercessor right in you— your Higher Self, your Holy Christ Self. You do not need an interpreter to talk to God, nor do you need anyone telling you when you are good enough to talk to God. God already gave you the gift of his presence.

DON'T CONDEMN YOURSELF

Don't condemn yourself for anything you have ever done. The devils have a heyday condemning you, but they have no right to condemn you. Accept God's judgments, not theirs.

Cast off their aggressive mental suggestion, which preys upon your mind and tells you that you are a terrible person who can never have any standing in the kingdom of God because of what you have done.

God can forgive any sin as long as the heart is penitent and humble and you are willing to make restitution, beginning with the violet flame that transmutes the record and the cause and core of the sin. God can forgive a murderer, a fornicator, a child abuser, anyone who is willing to remake his life and be converted to the very heart of God within. No matter how great or small the sin, never believe that it is a spot and a stain that cannot be transmuted by the sacred fire of seraphim.

HOW *to* WELCOME *the* SERAPHIM

Receive the seraphim, who come with the all-consuming fire of God. You can give them your filthy rags, your outworn garments. Let them clean out the attic of the mind and the basement of the subconscious and also the subbasement of the physical body.

If you can do so safely, you can periodically purge, cleanse, fast.[14] You can fast for a day on water or herbal tea, if you like. It's possible to fast and be a normal person. Nobody ever needs to know the holiness of God to which you aspire.

Talk to God in your heart. God has given you an altar, the secret chamber of your heart. The secret chamber of the heart is a dimension as vast as the whole cosmos and yet it is not even measurable in the physical sense of the word. Your soul can go there and commune with Christ, with the angels. That is where you whisper your deepest secrets, your greatest loves, your problems. Go to the altar of the heart.

Spiritually speaking, this is your interior castle, as Teresa of Avila called it. It is the place where you meet your God and your own Real Self. This is the inner walk of the mystics of every religion.

YOU CAN WALK *the* PATH *of* MYSTICISM

The inner teachings of this mystical path are what we must live and demonstrate so that the world can be freed from religion that has died. So much of religion has become rote and a dead ritual.

The world's major religions have two facets. The orthodox system of rituals provides what we need in terms of structure and rules and rituals. It is a religion of form. But a ritual is only meaningful when the minister is a flaming presence of light and can pour into that ritual the fire of God. When he does this, the ritual becomes a chalice to convey the light of the altar. When he does not, the ritual is empty. And so, as people advance on the spiritual path and become more sensitive to the light, they often discover that ritual alone is not enough. They want more.

Then there is the inner path of mysticism. Every one of the world's religions leads to the discovery that God is a living fire. Fire is the key in every religion from Zoroastrianism to Taoism to Christianity. The fire of the Holy Spirit, the flame, whatever way it is seen, is central on the altar of being. And the goal of the mystic is to unite with the flame, to unite with God—to be transformed, to be purged, to be illumined and to enter into total oneness.

The mystical path is a legitimate path. It is legitimate

to desire to be one with God. It is your divine birthright. All of the divine love of the universe is surrounding you now, intensifying in your being and telling you that this is the day and the hour when you can transcend yourself. That is why God sent us angels—they help us in the process of self-transcendence.

How do you transcend yourself? Just be a little bit better each day than you were the day before. Observe yourself and say, "I don't like the way I spoke to that person. I am going to watch my words more carefully and tomorrow my words will be kinder than they were today." Observe and self-correct, but don't become fanatical or rigid.

Work with the angels. Call to them often. Be willing to learn under Justinius and the seraphim. Pursue the holiness of God. Wear humility as an undergarment. Just be a normal person, not preaching to everyone you meet. Live what you believe in and go out of your way to help anyone in need.

Justinius says that in this way, "you are ascending moment by moment, erg by erg, as you give back to God the energy that he has given to you, as you give it back in good works, in word and deed and in the flow of the Holy Spirit, which you achieve magnificently by the science of the spoken Word and in your decrees."[15] Justinius says:

We march with all legions of every ray and every commander; for we are those who assist all angels to perform their tasks, including angels in embodiment such as you!

I bow to the light in each one. Whether it be a flicker of light or a veritable conflagration, I bow to the light as a single-drop candle flame.

Call to me at any hour of the night or day ... for you see, I am at the beck and call of Almighty God. And wherever I serve I must be aware of messengers of the Lord, of cosmic beings, of all in hierarchy —but above all of the voice of him before whose flame I bow even now, here in the plane of matter.[16]

COMMUNING *with the* SERAPHIM *and* ANGELS *of* VICTORY

MEET THE FIRE OF THE SERAPHIM

How do we meet the fire of the seraphim? We invoke the sacred fire through our mantras and decrees so that it is in our auras. We establish the fire around ourselves. If we do this, meeting the fire of the seraphim with this fire, we blend with and become congruent with their auras.

The angels of God surround his throne and perpetually sing to him, "Holy, holy, holy, Lord God Almighty. Thou art holy in manifestation in man!" If you give this affirmation, the angels will honor you and they will be with you even as they were with Jesus Christ, Moses, Buddha, and so many who have gone before us.

Holy, holy, holy, Lord God Almighty.
Thou art holy in manifestation in man!

When you give this affirmation, as simple as it is, it puts you in direct contact with the seraphim and cherubim of God—just by that very devotion of your heart.

CLAIM YOUR VICTORY

Mighty Victory says, "I come on wings of victory. I come to place the laurel wreath of victory upon the heads of the over-comers who are overcoming in all things, being tempted and tried yet still pressing on, dauntless toward the victory. These are they who are forging a new age.

"Come then. Come in your souls, O hearts of light. Affirm your victory, for you have had many victories of which you are not aware, that I acknowledge and affirm in the name of your God Self."[17]

Mighty Victory exhorts us to use this fiat to claim our victory:

In the name of Jesus the Christ and my own Christ Self,
In the name of the I AM THAT I AM,
I claim my victory now!
I claim my victory now!
I claim my victory now!

Notes

Unless otherwise specified, Bible references are to the King James Version. Throughout these notes, *PoW* is the abbreviation for *Pearls of Wisdom*.

Chapter 1 Angels and You
(**1**) Heb. 1:7. (**2**) Heb. 13:2. (**3**) Heb. 2:6–11. (**4**) John 14:12. (**5**) I Cor. 6:3. (**6**) See Hab. 1:13. (**7**) See John 14:23.

Chapter 2 How Angels Protect You and Those You Love
(**1**) See Exod. 3:13–14. (**2**) Dan. 12:1–2. (**3**) Dan. 12:3. (**4**) I Cor. 15:41. (**5**) Josh. 5:13–15. (**6**) Rev. 12:7–9. (**7**) Rev. 12:4. (**8**) *Saint Michael and the Angels* (Rockford, Ill.: Tan Books, 1983), p. 67. (**9**) Rev. 12:12. (**10**) Archangel Michael, "Meet Us Halfway!" July 5, 1992, in *PoW*, vol. 35, no. 50, November 8, 1992. (**11**) Deut. 6:4. (**12**) I Thess. 5:17. (**13**) The Goddess of Liberty, "The Keepers of the Flame of Liberty," July 5, 1986, in *PoW*, vol. 29, no. 65, November 23, 1986. (**14**) Archangel Michael's Rosary for Armageddon is a series of prayers, songs and decrees to Archangel Michael. It is available as a printed booklet and as an audio recording at www.SummitLighthouse .org. (**15**) Eph. 6:11, 14–17. (**16**) Rom. 10:13.

Chapter 3 How Angels Help You Contact Your Higher Self
(**1**) Acts 27:22–23 (New Jerusalem Bible). (**2**) Archangel Jophiel, "A Yellow Diamond Lodestone," October 9, 1971. (**3**) Phil. 2:5. (**4**) John 14:12. (**5**) Archangel Jophiel and Archeia Hope, "Is Anything Too Hard for the Lord?" July 2, 1989, in *PoW*, vol. 32, no. 36, September 3, 1989. (**6**) Archangel Jophiel and Christine, March 26, 1989, in *PoW*, vol. 32, no. 22, May 28, 1989. (**7**) Archangel Jophiel, "An Era of Unprecedented Enlightenment," January 1, 1989, in *PoW*, vol. 32, no. 5, January 29, 1989. (**8**) Archeia Christine, "New Age Teaching Methods," July 1, 1973, in *PoW*, vol. 16, no. 49, December 9, 1973.

Chapter 4 How Angels Help You Experience More Love
(**1**) John 13:34–35. (**2**) Gal. 5:14. (**3**) Gen. 3:24. (**4**) Exod. 25:20, 21–22. (**5**) J. Coert Rylaarsdam, exegesis on the Book of Exodus, *The Interpreter's Bible* (Nashville, Tenn.: Abingdon Press, 1980), 1:1024. (**6**) Ezek. 1:4–5, 13. (**7**) Among the books recommended by Mrs. Prophet on the healing of the inner child are *Your Inner Child of the Past,* by W. Hugh Missildine; *Healing Your Aloneness,* by Erika Chopich and Margaret Paul; *Inner Bonding,* by Margaret Paul; *The Inner Child Workbook,* by Cathryn L. Taylor; and *Healing the Child Within,* by Charles L. Whitfield. (**8**) Archangel Chamuel and Charity, "Keys to the Twelve Gates of the Celestial City," February 14, 1986, in *PoW*, vol. 29, no. 26, June 11, 1986. (**9**) Heb. 12:6. (**10**) Archangel Chamuel, "Be Gone, Forces of Anti-Love!" October 4, 1992, in *PoW*, vol. 35, no. 58, November 29, 1992. (**11**) Chapter 5 of the Book of Genesis gives the names and ages of a number of those who lived before the Flood of Noah (the sinking of the continent of Atlantis). The longest lifespan recorded there is that of Methuselah, who lived to the age of 969. (**12**) Archangel Chamuel, "Be Gone, Forces of Anti-Love!" (**13**) Ibid.

Chapter 5 How Angels Help You Recapture the Spirit of Joy
(**1**) Archangel Gabriel, "The Hope of the Mother and her Children,"

October 10, 1977. (**2**) Archangel Gabriel, "The Annunciation of Your Soul's Victory," May 3, 1991, in *PoW,* vol. 34, no. 27, June 25, 1991. (**3**) Archangel Gabriel, "The Father's Message of Your Salvation unto Him," May 24, 1986, in *PoW,* vol. 29, no. 54, November 6, 1986. (**4**) Archangel Gabriel, "The Joy of the Path," April 20, 1984, in *PoW,* vol. 27, no. 30, June 4, 1984. (**5**) John 15:11. (**6**) Archangel Gabriel, "Called to an Unusual Sacrifice," October 2, 1987, in *PoW,* vol. 30, no. 53, November 22, 1987. (**7**) Archangel Gabriel, "The Judgment of Love," February 15, 1986, in *PoW,* vol. 29, no. 31, June 22, 1986. (**8**) Archangel Gabriel, "Annunciation of Your Soul's Victory." (**9**) Archangel Gabriel and Hope, "Sendings of the Sacred Fire," December 31, 1980, in *PoW,* vol. 24, no. 9, March 1, 1981. (**10**) Archeia Hope, "The Eternal Now Is My Hope," January 2, 1987, in *PoW,* vol. 30, no. 4, January 25, 1987. (**11**) Ibid. (**12**) Ibid.

Chapter 6 How Angels Help You Heal Yourself and Others
(**1**) See Tobit 6, 11, 12. (**2**) Archangel Raphael, "The Day of the Coming of the Lord's Angel: Healing, Karma, and the Path," February 16, 1986, in *PoW,* vol. 29, no. 32, June 29, 1986. (**3**) Archangel Raphael, "A Healing Matrix: The Crystal of the Fifth Ray of Elohim," June 29, 1988, in *PoW,* vol. 31, no. 56, September 3, 1988; Archangel Raphael and Mother Mary, "Healing, Karma, and the Violet Flame," February 8, 1987, in *PoW,* vol. 30, no. 7, February 15, 1987. (**4**) Archangel Raphael and Mother Mary, "Healing, Karma, and Violet Flame." (**5**) Archangel Raphael, "Coming of the Lord's Angel." (**6**) See John 9:4, 5; 12:35, 36. (**7**) Archangel Raphael, "Coming of the Lord's Angel." (**8**) Archangel Raphael and Mother Mary, "Healing, Karma, and Violet Flame." (**9**) Ibid. (**10**) M. R. James, trans., *The Apocryphal New Testament* (Oxford Clarendon Press, 1924). (**11**) Mother Mary, "Marriage in the Church Universal and Triumphant," December 24, 1983, in *PoW,* vol. 27, no. 2, January 8, 1984; "Behold the Handmaid (Shakti) of the Lord!" December 31, 1977; "Good Friday: The Betrayal and the Victory," April 1, 1983, in *PoW,* vol. 26, no. 28, July 10, 1983.

Chapter 7 How Angels Help You Create Personal and Planetary Change
(**1**) "The Best and Worst of Everything," *Parade Magazine,* January 5, 1986, p. 4. (**2**) James H. Charlesworth, ed., *The Old Testament Pseudepigrapha* (Garden City, N.Y.: Doubleday & Co., 1983), pp. 350–51. (**3**) Exod. 14:13. (**4**) Archangel Uriel, "'Thus Far and No Farther!' Saith the LORD," December 29, 1985, in *PoW,* vol. 29, no. 16, April 20, 1986. (**5**) Chris Merkel, "Cave-In!" *Guideposts,* February 1993, pp. 25–27. (**6**) Archangel Uriel, "'Thus Far and No Farther!'" (**7**) Archangel Uriel, "A Sense of Destiny in the Cosmic Stream of History," May 25, 1986, in *PoW,* vol. 29, no. 56, November 8, 1986. (**8**) Archangel Uriel, "'The Hour for the Fulfillment of Your Christhood," February 27, 1988, in *PoW,* vol. 31, no. 36, July 6, 1988. (**9**) See *The Science of the Spoken Word,* by Mark L. Prophet and Elizabeth Clare Prophet, for full color thoughtforms showing how you can visualize the violet flame, the resurrection flame, and the healing thoughtform over different organs. (Summit University Press, 2004.) (**10**) Archangel Uriel, "I Deliver the Purging Light to Pierce Your Rebellion Against God," part 1, July 7, 1991, in *PoW,* vol. 48, no. 12, March 20, 2005. (**11**) Archangel Uriel and Aurora, "The Hour of Justice Is Come," July 5, 1992, in *PoW,* vol. 35, no. 55, November 21, 1992. (**12**) Archangel Uriel, "Overcome by the Power of Light!" March 30, 1983, in *PoW,* vol. 26, no. 23, June 5, 1983. (**13**) Archangel Uriel,

"The Sealing of This Cycle of the Lord's Resurrection," April 15, 1979. (**14**) Archangel Uriel, "Walk the Earth as Christs!" July 4, 1966, in *PoW,* vol. 25, no. 50, December 12, 1982. (**15**) Ibid.

Chapter 8 How Angels Help You Create Miracles in Your Life

(**1**) Archangel Zadkiel, "The Joy of Judgment in the Flame of Transmutation," in Elizabeth Clare Prophet, *Vials of the Seven Last Plagues* (Gardiner, Mont.: Summit University Press, 2004), p. 90. (**2**) *Merriam-Webster's Collegiate Dictionary,* 11th ed., s.v. "alchemy." (**3**) Saint Germain, "The Harvest," December 2, 1984, in *PoW,* vol. 27, no. 61, December 23, 1984. (**4**) Archangel Zadkiel, "The Sealing of the Seventh Ray," December 30, 1980, in *PoW,* vol. 24, no. 6, February 8, 1981. (**5**) Prophet and Prophet, *Science of the Spoken Word,* p. 158. (**6**) Archangel Zadkiel, "My Gift of the Violet Flame," October 6, 1987, in *PoW,* vol. 30, no. 58, November 27, 1987. (**7**) I Cor. 15:41. (**8**) Matt. 6:20. (**9**) Archangel Zadkiel, April 5, 1969. (**10**) *Saint Germain On Alchemy* (Gardiner, Mont.: Summit University Press, 2011), pp. 3–4. (**11**) Elizabeth Clare Prophet, *How to Work with Angels* (Gardiner, Mont.: Summit University Press, 1998), p. 91. (**12**) Archangel Zadkiel, March 24, 1989, in *PoW,* vol. 32, no. 17, April 23, 1989. (**13**) Archangel Zadkiel and Holy Amethyst, "Go Forth and Do Battle with the Goliath of the Modern Superstate," December 30, 1974, in *PoW,* vol. 52, no. 21, November 1, 2009. (**14**) Archangel Zadkiel, March 24, 1989. (**15**) Ibid. (**16**) Archangel Zadkiel, "Gift of the Violet Flame."

Chapter 9 How to Meet Your Guardian Angel

(**1**) Matt. 18:10. (**2**) Elaine H. Pagels, *The Johannine Gospel in Gnostic Exegesis: Heracleon's Commentary on John* (reprint; Atlanta, Ga.: Scholars Press, 1989), p. 80. (**3**) Peter Lamborn Wilson, *Angels* (New York: Pantheon Books, 1980), p. 102. (**4**) *Saint Michael and the Angels,* p. 36. (**5**) Valentine Long, *The Angels in Religion and Art* (Chicago: Franciscan Herald Press, 1970), p. 97. (**6**) II Hermas VI:7, 9, 10, 12, *The Apocryphal New Testament* (London: William Hone, 1820). (**7**) Gloria G. Gibson, "Angels Everywhere," *Catholic Digest,* February 1992, p. 55. (**8**) Ibid, p. 56. (**9**) Colleen Smith Mason, "All About Angels," *Catholic Digest,* April 1991, p. 44. (**10**) Pope John XXIII, quoted in Bob and Penny Lord, *Heavenly Army of Angels* (Journeys of Faith, 1991), p. 48.

Chapter 10 How to Work with Angels for Success

(**1**) Justinius, "The Saturation of Light," May 15, 1988, in *PoW,* vol. 31, no. 54, August 27, 1988. (**2**) Justinius, June 2, 1974. (**3**) Justinius, "The Saturation of Light." (**4**) III Enoch 26:9–11, Charlesworth, *Old Testament Pseudepigrapha,* p. 281. (**5**) Isa. 6:1–8 (King James Version and Jerusalem Bible). (**6**) Enzo Orlandi, ed., *The Life and Times of St. Francis* (Philadelphia: Curtis Publishing Co., 1967), p. 63. (**7**) Mary Baker Eddy, *Science and Health with Key to the Scriptures* (Boston: First Church of Christ, Scientist, 1875), p. 581. (**8**) See Gen. 14:18–20; Heb. 7:1–2. (**9**) Mighty Victory, "A Spiral for Christ Victory," December 29, 1974, in *PoW,* vol. 43, no. 13, March 26, 2000. (**10**) Mighty Victory, "Always Victory!" January 2, 1989, in *PoW,* vol. 32, no. 7, February 12, 1989. (**11**) Mighty Victory, "Indomitable Greetings of Cosmic Victory," January 3, 1971, in *PoW,* vol. 19, no. 45, November 7, 1976. (**12**) Mighty Victory, "The Circle of Fire," March 3, 1974, in *PoW,* vol. 43, no. 11, March 12, 2000. (**13**) Mighty Victory, "Indomitable Greetings." (**14**) Some recommendations concerning fasting: Never fast if you are pregnant or a nursing mother. If you have a medical or mental health condition, consult your doctor before fasting. Fasting for more than three days is not recommended unless you consult a health professional. If you feel lightheaded or disoriented or if you become ill while fasting, stop your fast and gradually return to solid foods. (15) Justinius, "The Army of the Hosts of the Lord," March 6, 1977. (16) Justinius, "The Will to Win," March 28, 1991, in *PoW*, vol. 34, no. 17, April 28, 1991; Justinius, "The Saturation of Light"; Justinius, June 2, 1974. (17) Mighty Victory, "Spiral for Christ Victory."

Illustrations

1: *Angels Looking over Jerusalem.* **2:** *Saint John the Evangelist's Vision of Jerusalem,* Alonzo Cano. **9:** The Chart of Your Divine Self. **14:** The Seven Major Chakras. **24:** *The Knight of the Holy Grail* (detail), Frederick J. Waugh. **27:** *Saint Michael,* Domenico Ghirlandaio. **28:** *Apparition of Sts. Michael Archangel and Catherine to Joan of Arc* (left-side of *The Life of Joan of Arc* triptych), Hermann Anton Stilke. **37:** *An Angel Appears to the Israelites,* Gustave Doré. **38:** *The Fall of the Rebel Angels,* from *Très Riches Heures du Duc de Berry,* Limbourg brothers. **44:** *St. Michael Vanquishing Satan,* Raphael. **59:** *The Dream of Saint Joseph* (detail), Philippe de Champaigne. **60:** *Archangel Uriel* (stained glass window), Tiffany Studios. **64:** *The Liberation of St. Peter* (detail), Raphael. **71:** *The Inspiration of St. Matthew,* Caravaggio. **72:** The Angel Isrâfîl. **81:** Angel from *The Resurrection of Jesus Christ* (polyptych), Titian. **82:** *Charity* (mosaic). **87:** Replica of the Ark of the Covenant, George Washington Masonic National Memorial; photo by Ben Schumin, creativecommons.org/licenses/by-sa/2.5. **90:** *Adam and Eve Driven Out of Eden,* Gustave Doré. **109:** *The Annunciation: The Angel Gabriel* (detail), Gaudenzio Ferrari. **110:** Archangel Gabriel (stained glass window). **114:** *The Annunciation* (detail), Leonardo da Vinci. **119:** *Mohammed the Prophet* 1932 (detail), Nicholas Roerich. **129:** *Abraham and the Three Angels* (detail), Gerbrand van den Eeckhout. **130:** *The Archangel and Tobias,* unknown Lombard painter, 17th cent. **135:** *The Three Archangels with Tobias* (detail), Francesco Botticini. **138:** *Virgin of the Globe.* **143:** *The Virgin with Angels,* William-Adolphe Bougereau. **147:** *The Annunciation* (detail), Philippe de Champaigne. **150:** The Healing Thoughtform. **155:** St. Uriel (mosaic), St. John's Church, Boreham, Wiltshire. **156:** *Angel,* Abbott Handerson Thayer. **159:** *The Last Angel* 1942 (detail), Nicholas Roerich. **164:** *Angels* (detail), Benozzo Gozzoli. **175:** *The Days of Creation—The First Day* (detail), Edward Burne-Jones. **179:** *Angel with Trumpet* (stained glass window). **180:** *Agony in the Garden,* Giulio Cesare Procaccini. **186:** *The Sacrifice of Isaac,* workshop of Rembrandt. **191:** *Francis of Assisi in Ecstasy* (detail), Caravaggio. **203:** *Sir Galahad and His Angel,* Noel Paton. **204:** Eighteenth Century painting of a guardian angel, artist unknown. **208:** *Angel Appearing to St. Jerome,* Guido Reni. **213:** *Saint Bernard and the Guardian Angel,* Jaume Huguet. **221:** *Isaiah's Lips Anointed with Fire* (detail), Benjamin West. **222:** *Stigmatization of St. Francis,* Giotto. **226:** *Angels in Heaven,* Gustave Doré. **233:** *The Empyrean* (highest heaven), Gustave Doré.

The Summit Lighthouse®

63 Summit Way

Gardiner, Montana 59030 USA

1-800-245-5445 / 406-848-9500

Se habla espanol.

TSLinfo@TSL.org

SummitLighthouse.org

Elizabeth Clare Prophet (1939–2009) was a pioneer of modern spirituality and an internationally renowned speaker and author. Her books are published in more than 30 languages, and millions of copies have been sold online and in bookstores worldwide.

Throughout her lifetime, Mrs. Prophet walked the path of spiritual adeptship, advancing through the universal initiations common to mystics of both East and West. She taught about this path and described her own experiences for the benefit of all who desire to make spiritual progress.

Mrs. Prophet has left an extensive library of spiritual teachings from the ascended masters and a thriving, worldwide community of people who study and practice these teachings.